I0022131

SILHOUETTES OF STRATEGIES FROM AUTHENTIC COACHES FOR MIND, BODY, & SOUL

VISIONARY: MICHELLE BOULDEN-HAMMOND

FOREWORD BY: DR. MARY J. HUNTLEY

COPYRIGHT 2020© MICHELLE BOULDEN HAMMOND. ALL RIGHTS RESERVED.

Written and Created by Visionary Author Michelle Boulden-Hammond with Contributing Co- Authors: Bernadette Brawner, Joi Brown, Kyonna F. Brown, Dr. Jennifer Jones Bryant, Sheila Gibson, Shawna Halley, Victoria Holland, Pastor Mike Kabia, Lynda D. Mallory, Charlene Harrod-Owuamana, Milagros Richards and Foreword Written By Dr. Mary J. Huntley.

Published By: A Life With A View Publishing

Copyright Disclaimer

This book or parts thereof may not be reproduced in any form, stored in a retrieval system, or transmitted in any form such as photocopied, recorded, mechanical or electronic, otherwise without prior written permission of the publisher, except as provided by the United States of America copyright law.

Biblical Reference unless otherwise noted, scripture reference is taken from the King James Version of the Holy Bible.

Tables of Contents

A Letter from the Publisher 1

FOREWORD: 2

Visionary Introduction 6

Chapter 1: Relationships/ Financial Wellness **8**

YOUR RELATIONSHIPS AND FINANCES MATTER 9

RESTORING THE BROKEN PIECES 14

Chapter 2: Health Fitness Wellness Coaches **22**

BECOMING A HEALTHIER YOU – "THE TRANSFORMATION 23

THE HEARTBEAT OF WATER 30

Health and Fitness 39

Chapter 3: Professional Development **43**

Beware of Coaching Hustlers! 44

Chapter 4: Personal Development Rocks **52**

Speak Life into HerStory 53

Overcoming to Elevate 60

Chapter 5: Spiritual Soul Wellness Coaches **67**

Shifting Gears With Grace 68

God's Timing Is Always Perfect 73

MEET THE AUTHORS 78

Special Thanks 101

A Letter from the Publisher

For the last 7 years since 2013, I have had the pleasure of collaborating and working with some amazing people who have become part of the A Life with A View family. I am honored to be in this space going from blogger, to author, to now a publisher. This is no accident; this winding road journey and how this all came about.

In January 2016, I attended an event in Washington, DC and I met Michelle Hammond. Michelle won a copy of my first book, *A Life with A View*, and since then we have stayed in touch, we have become great friends and partners on this book collaboration and publishing journey. When Michelle asked me to be part of her book publishing team, I was thrilled and very happy to work on this amazing project with her and some of the great people she has come to know while following and fulfilling her life's purpose.

And to our *Silhouettes*, you are in great hands with Michelle and her caring spirit. She has brought us far in this journey and with your amazing expertise, you continue to help and inspire other people. I encourage you to keep going and help each other along the way. You are forever together, bound by this beautiful collaboration, and continue to go forth, be great, and be your absolute best.

With Love Always,

Lynda D. Mallory

A Life with A View Publishing

www.lyndadmallory.com

FOREWORD:

Silhouettes of Strategies From Authentic Coaches For Mind, Body, & Soul

It is my distinct privilege to pen the Foreword for Silhouettes of Strategies From Authentic Coaches For Mind, Body, and Soul. Award winning, bestselling author and visionary Michelle Boulden-Hammond is credentialed through one of the top coaching organizations, the International Coaching Federation, as a life coach. She has a plethora of first-hand knowledge regarding the "do's and don'ts of coaching. Additionally, her warm, contagious smile and charismatic personality are assets that help clients reach their desired results. Like other industries, the coaching industry can be laced with wolves dressed in sheep clothing. Michelle has selected amazing co-authors to share various coaching niches, including health and wellness, finance, professional development, spirituality, and relationships.

Coaching can be described as a partnership with clients to help them grow, reach their goals or desired results, or become unstuck. Presently, Life Coaching is an extremely exciting and lucrative industry. Because of COVID-19's worldwide devastation, it will definitively remain in high demand. Losses have devastated families worldwide. No one saw COVID's devastation coming down the pipeline and it was not forecast. Therefore, there was no planning or preparation time. In spite of this, the number of coaches in the U.S. continues to grow, as consumers seek advice and motivation shifting & pivoting in their careers, classes and so much more. The huge need for coaches is a result of hundreds of thousands of losses. The losses involve loved ones, jobs, relationships, pets, or finances.

Not only is coaching a fast-growing industry, but according to the U.S. Department of Labor, the number of life coaches employed in the United States is expected to grow 21% by 2022 according to Health Coach Institute. The average salaries of life coaches are estimated to range from $50K-$75K, with the top 10% of coaches earning $100K. The coaching industry has a wide variety of specialties otherwise known as niches. A few of the specialties are executive leadership, career, business, finance, relationship, health, wellness, divorce, loss, grief, and temperament. The specialties allow coaches to navigate the specific lane where the client has a need. Various creative processes may be utilized to empower and inspire clients to maximize their potential. The return on investment is usually far greater when utilizing a specialist. Coaching is a market with few barriers and several organizations certifying students for various fees. However, "let the buyer beware" this industry's lack of stringent regulation has drawn criticism.

I recently became a part of a cohort of aspiring women speakers. It took more than thinking about it; I had to show up, speak up and follow up to receive my certification. I had to produce during our sessions that lasted one year. Our class went through rigorous training to acquire this well sought-after certification from an international master speaker development coach and empowerment guru. She made it noticeably clear that we would earn our keeps; and that we did. The lessons learned, gems, jewels, nuggets, and handouts were invaluable, and well worth the investment. I am much more confident that this certification in conjunction with my board-certified master life coach credentials will empower me to serve my clients on a different professional level. And I am aware that it is not only about certifications. However, it is about being called, equipped, and empowered to serve my clients in excellence.

My clients deserve my best not leftovers. I never want anyone to feel that I am ill prepared to serve them. Therefore, I felt the need to add credentials to my personal life-coaching arsenal. I am grateful for certifications in health & wellness, relationship, marriage, addiction & recovery, executive & organizational, and temperament life coaching. As a professional change agent, I am genuinely committed to help each client. It is my endeavor to build a healthy relationship with each one. This includes a relationship built upon trust by both parties. My level of commitment is especially important to each client. That commitment does not come from a particular technique or experience; but it comes from the depths of my very being. I honestly believe and join the leadership guru John Maxwell in saying "people do not care how much you know until they know how much you care."

When seeking a professional coach, you should conduct proper research to include credentials, which allows us to see what institution, or organization authorizes, supports, and stands behind the coach's training and credentials. In essence, having legal and legitimate credentials attached to one's name provides credence to their deliverables. Some organizations require recertification during various intervals. Another part of one's research when seeking a professional coach should include niche or specialty training, experience, and references. Ask clarifying questions about the benefits of working with a particular coach. If you do not conduct proper research "let the buyer beware", you may get a mixed bag of foolery. It is not unusual to see "pop up coaches." Unfortunately, some of these individuals have taken a quick course over the internet, paid the fee, and now call themselves coach. In some cases, they have simply pondered over how they can get a fast buck; so, they speak with a few individuals and label themselves coach.

Silhouettes of Strategies from Authentic Coaches, For the Mind, Body & Soul addresses various coaching topics. These intriguing silhouettes provide a sneak preview into the reality of the coaching world and industry. The readers take a step into the coach's office to witness grace in motion. Life is sometimes filled with sudden turns, bumps, curves, detours, and stop signs. We do not always get warnings, nor is there a huge neon sign flashing ahead. However, it is crucial that we shift gears appropriately and navigate the turns to arrive at our correct destination. Shifting gears is a very gingerly movement; we must shift with grace. Another co-author cautions us about self-proclaimed coaches. They may come dressed in executive suits, with amazing articulation of speech, and they may come highly recommended. However, it is paramount that we conduct our research to ensure that we are not "taken" by some of these fly-by-night hustlers. On the other hand, some may be well meaning, however, they are ill equipped to produce the deliverables. They can do more harm than good. When we rush the process of conducting proper research "let the buyer beware." You may short-change yourself. Therefore, do not abort the process!

One seasoned, credentialed coach/co-author shares powerful very salient inappropriate coaches' behavior that should always raise a red flag. She has enumerated the behavior and articulated each point in a very compelling manner. Her information will empower you to avoid some wolves dressed in sheep clothing. Coaches should always uphold the "confidentiality" agreement. Under no circumstances should this be violated.

These stories are written with authenticity and specific strategies to empower the reader and to provide a sneak preview and a look into the huge, growing coaching industry that lacks stringent regulations. This amazing collaboration will allow you to embrace various truths for the mind, body, and soul; as well as provide a well-rounded view into the coaching industry.

Thank you for joining us as we explore Silhouettes of Strategies From Authentic Coaches For Mind, Body, and Soul. Our awesome, bestselling author and award-winning visionary has charted an amazing course for your reading pleasure and edification. Now that I have aroused your suspicion, piqued your interest, and whet your appetite, I encourage you to fasten your seatbelt, relax, and enjoy!

Dr. Mary J. Huntley

Board-Certified Master Life Coach

2019 Indie Author Legacy Award Winner

Master Motivational Mindset Coach

3X International Bestselling Author

8X Bestselling Author

www.drmaryjhuntley.com

Visionary Introduction

Michelle Boulden-Hammond

The book *Silhouettes of Strategies From Authentic Coaches for Mind, Body & Soul* is a collection of shared expertise from some amazing authentic coaches from various sectors that include: Health & Fitness, Personal Growth & Development, Professional Development, Relationships, Finances, and Spiritual Soul Wellness. You as the reader at this very moment have received this book of instructions not by choice, but as a divine special delivery ordained for such a time as now. An essential tool if you are looking to become a certified coach or you may just want to go on a self-discovery journey in finding the real you. As you see the real you must be ***Authentic!*** You may ask the question what does authentic mean? Merriam Webster has some great definitions for the word authentic. One definition states: *worthy of acceptance or belief as conforming to or based on fact.* So, what kind of picture are you painting if you are a coach or looking to explore the coaching field? Another definition for the word authentic states: *not false or imitation.* The only imitation we need to be is of Christ as it is clearly noted in scripture reference Ephesians 5:1 - Therefore be imitators of God, as beloved children. Will the real you please stand up?

We know that we can say that truly we had no idea when we thought about coming into the year of 2020 that we would have a whirlwind of events such as a national pandemic, racial divide and changes after changes. However, as for me I will say that this pandemic has brought me more in tune with my gift of coaching and inspiring others. I am now going to be transparent for a bit just to let you know that this journey has not happened as a one hit wonder of overnight success. My journey began over twelve years ago in the field of coaching. I was trained through the International Coaching Federation and one thing that was drilled is the Code of Ethics and the Integrity Statement. You could say that this was the official governed laws to use as being a professional in the coaching field. The one rule of thumb is to DO NO HARM! So here you have it my dear reader. This powerful resource was inspired during the pandemic by God to release and intensify some true and authentic coaches. I have clearly watched people being misused and abused by coaches or supposed to be coaches being swindled out of thousands of dollars and not finishing projects. Where has the integrity gone? Another transparent moment I have been a victim as well. I am a firm believer that things happen for a reason. I have learned the strategy of making every negative encounter and changing it to the mode of positive.

As I stated earlier, when I started out as a coach over twelve years ago, I moved graciously by hosting open women empowerment day conferences. There were no social media pages followers just word of mouth. Today I still have the consistency of people who started with me from the beginning and that is because I have truly been authentic and genuine from the beginning. Clearly, there has been no harm done along my journey as a Personal Development Growth & Health and Wellness Diabetes Self – Management coach through the CDC Lifestyle Coach Program. In my service as a coach, I have been recognized for helping corporate companies receive Maryland Healthiest Business Awards for outstanding coaching measures. I give God all the glory for him working through me to be a change of connection of helping people with coaching needs professionally and personally. There may be more questions than answers in finding and defining the true authentic self, but always remind yourself that integrity matters and always remain ethical in the process of coaching. So here I have selected some powerful authentic coaches to give you some insights for your self-discovery journey for a new you. I want to give you some common characteristics that you must adhere to in being an authentic Certified Coach:

1. You must be accepting of yourself and of other people
2. Thoughtful
3. Realistic perception of making things a reality
4. Open to learning from mistakes
5. Being able to understand your motivations
6. Able to express emotions clearly and free

In closing this book called *Silhouettes of Strategies From Authentic Coaches for Mind, Body & Soul,* my prayer is that you embark on this journey of alignment and undergo the process to move forward in your desired measures of being a certified coach or being coached.

Beginnings

Chapter 1

RELATIONSHIPS/ FINANCIAL WELLNESS

YOUR RELATIONSHIPS AND FINANCES MATTER

Bernadette M. Brawner

How many of you can honestly say that you are in a healthy relationship? Immediately, what did you first think about after reading this question? Was it the relationship with your spouse, significant other; child, family member, or friend?

We have all experienced some healthy and unhealthy relationships in our lifetime. How many of you can remember your first real and healthy relationship? Yes, let us think about this for a moment. I am not going to take for granted that the reader's answer is their first relationship is with their mother or father because this may not be the case. I want you to think about this and be honest with yourself. I do understand that some of us must dig deep to find this answer. Mainly because I purposefully put in the question, "healthy" due to the lack of this type of relationship may not exist or has vanished for some reason or another.

Let us take a closer look at the definition of "relationship" and correspond it to what we have grown to believe what this word means to us now. I googled the definition, and it states:

- the state of being connected by blood or marriage; or
- the way in which two or more people or groups regard and behave toward each other.

I would like to share some characteristics of a healthy relationship verses an unhealthy relationship that you can use to assess what type of relationship you are currently in which will aid with your decision to leave or stay whether it is a personal or business. I would like to point out that it all starts with LOVE, yes love. ***What's LOVE has to do with it? Love is a major factor and ingredient in all RELATIONSHIPS.***

The Bible's definition of love should be the compass for measuring what love is or means to oneself. After all, you were made with love, God's Love. Let me remind you what the Bible says in 1 Corinthians 13. This verse provides us with what should be accepted and not accepted when it comes to love and relationship.

In summary, LOVE IS....

- ✓ Patient
- ✓ Kind
- ✓ Rejoices in truth
- ✓ Bears up under all problems/protects
- ✓ Believes/Trusts
- ✓ Hopes
- ✓ Understands the faults of other
- ✓ Never fails/Perseveres

LOVE IS NOT....

- ✓ Envious
- ✓ Proud
- ✓ Boastful
- ✓ Inappropriate/Rude
- ✓ Selfish
- ✓ Short-tempered
- ✓ Evil
- ✓ Accepting of sin

Now we cannot have a conversation about relationships without looking inward. I want to bring your attention to the most important relationship that you should have and that is one with yourself. Have you ever taken that time to assess the importance of self-love? How about your needs and wants to be in a healthy relationship? I find that majority of the time, we look to others to make us happy or sustain a relationship. Relying on others to make us happy is not the way to live.

According to Psychology Today – Self-love is not simply a state of feeling good. It is a state of appreciation for oneself that *grows from actions* that support our physical, psychological, and spiritual growth. Self-love is dynamic; it grows through actions that mature us. When we act in ways that expand self-love in us, we begin to accept much better our weaknesses as well as our strengths; less need to explain away our shortcomings, have compassion for ourselves as human beings struggling to find personal meaning, are more centered in our life purpose and values, and expect living fulfillment through our own efforts.

Here are Seven Keys to Self-Love:

- ✓ Become mindful
- ✓ Act on what you need rather than what you want
- ✓ Practice good self-care
- ✓ Set boundaries
- ✓ Protect yourself
- ✓ Forgive yourself
- ✓ Live intentionally

You see, a healthy relationship between two or more people incudes YOU. Ensuring that you are stable and healthy is necessary to have a successful relationship with others. When our relationships are healthy, everything around us flows. Relationships are like that of a gardener planting flowers. Our connections to self and others are like planting flowers. Relationships allow us to plant seeds, cultivate, water, and grow in every aspect of our lives.

I would like to illustrate three simple steps for you to take when building and sustaining a relationship. While these steps may seem easy, it does require some work from you. Do I have any gardeners reading this chapter? Ok, let us look at the process of gardening and planting a seed and compare it to your relationship. What are three things a plant needs to grow? **SOIL, SUNLIGHT**, and **WATER**. Just as a plant needs these things to grow, so do relationships. Oh, do not forget about the **WEEDS**. When you are planning to grow, these are the necessities:

1. **Soil** – The soil is a necessity for plants to grow. It serves as the foundation to the start of life. **Ephesians 3:17** tells us that we are to be rooted and grounded in the Love of Christ. Just as the plant needs nutrients from rich soil to thrive, so do our relationships. Our nutrients are Peace, Love, Encouragement, and Wisdom.
2. **Sunlight** – Plants need sunlight to grow. We need the energy from others to foster good relationships. Without any light, our lives would be lifeless. Sunlight comes in the form

of a smile, a helping hand, a lifeline, forgiveness, laughter, making time for others, integrity, grit, and sisterhood to name a few.

3. **Water** – Finally yet importantly, plants need water to grow and to sustain them. Our water is in the form of fellowship with others and fellow believers. God did not intend for us to be alone nor grow alone. It is impossible. We need each other and to encourage one another. You see **1 Thessalonians 5:11** tells us "Therefore encourage one another and build one another up, just as you are doing." **Proverbs 27:17** also states, "Iron sharpens iron, and one man sharpens another." Fellowship is so refreshing to the soul. It is like water to a plant. It can perk us up when we had a bad day or can quench our thirst. Water is the vessel for the nutrient we need to grow. **Matthew 18:20** tells us that for where two or three are gathered in my name, I am there during them.

You see relationships are vital to our lives. It is what makes us who we are and striving to be in life. Now that we have talked about the essentials, do not forget about the weeds. Just like plants have weeds, so do relationships. **Weeds** come in all shapes, colors, and forms. While other weeds, like wayward friends or feelings of bitterness and anger, can be hard to keep away. Weeds choke plants, creating an atmosphere where growth can be impossible. Weeds work in our lives much the same way in relationships. They distract us and can crush smaller, weaker plants easily just as some may do in relationships.

Continue to strengthen yourselves with good soil, sunlight, and refreshing water by this you will find yourself strong roots that is deeply rooted in your foundation and your relationships will flourish. As you cultivate your relationship with others let us chat about your relationship with money. How are you doing in this area? Did you know that your perspective on money has a lot to do with your personal relationship, your exposure to financial literacy, and triggers? Believe it or not, your relationship with money stems from what you were taught as a child or the lack thereof.

When I think about my young adult childhood, I do not recall being taught about finances. Do you? In fact, talking about money then and now has always been taboo. I used to wonder why but now I know. Lack of knowledge in this area is the culprit. We were taught to get our education and graduate from high school, but no special emphasis was put on learning budgeting, saving, or investing. Also, the more I think about it, some of us grew up poor, so money was not on the forefront of our minds. We were trying to survive and make sure our bills were paid. There was hardly any extra money left to save or invest.

This experience became my triggers in adulthood. I remember making it a point not to have anything to do with money. I was afraid to educate myself about money. Then people that valued their finances were hired as an entry-level professional in budgeting surrounded me; and my life changed for the better. Once I learned the concepts, studied, and opened my eyes to financial literacy I became fond of this topic. Not only did I become educated in this topic, I also paid attention to my triggers surrounding my finances and what made me overspend and not stay on task. Know your triggers, when they occur, and how to mitigate them. You will be successful when handling your finances if you become acquainted with your money.

I am happy to share that I am now on a mission to educate individuals on the importance of relationships whether it is personal, professional, or with their finances (aka money). I am a certified life coach with a focus on personal development and finances. I shift the mindsets of individuals that want to become debt free and live a life of freedom. I am ready to walk this journey with you one step at a time until you are comfortable, confident, and courageous enough to change. Why? Because YOUR RELATIONSHIPS AND FINANCES MATTER!!

Tips for a great relationship

"The journey of a thousand miles begins with a single step". – *Lao-tzu*

✓ Surround yourself around a community of people who inspire you
✓ Believe in yourself, appreciate who you are, dream and create
✓ Collaborate! Collaborate! Collaborate!
✓ Come together, celebrate each other, and share your stories and the desires of the heart
✓ Complement others
✓ Support and uplift each other
✓ Listen
✓ Be Confident
✓ Encourage one another
✓ Emit positive energy
✓ Laugh together, regularly ☺
✓ Show Love and Gratitude

RESTORING THE BROKEN PIECES

Sheila Gibson

Palms 143:8: Cause me to hear thy loving kindness in the morning; for in thee do I trust: Cause me to know the way wherein I should walk; for I lift up my soul unto thee.

You have no idea how God will send you a blessing. **John 15:12**: This is my commandment, that ye love one another, as I have loved you. One day, I was with my sister and she was sharing how a friend of her cousin expecting a child. She mentioned she and her husband would be taking custody when she gives birth. My sister then tells me that my friend who will take custody her cousin's baby, now they have found out their daughter is expecting and they are not going to help her cousin. So, I say to my sister this was a horrible situation. In conversation, I stated to my sister if that was me, I would have helped with the baby.

A few days later, I was at work and my phone rang. It was a stranger who asked for me, and I said "this is she?" She then said: "can you come to Greater South East Hospital in Washington, DC?" I said what is wrong she said I can't discuss it over with you over the phone. In a panic, I left my job and drove straight to the hospital. In my mind, I thought something happened to my kids or family member. Upon my arrival, I went to the information desk to give them my name. They directed me to the fifth floor and asked for Ms. Naomi. I got off the elevator when I approached the desk it seems like they were waiting for my arrival. I said: "hello I received a call to come here because it was urgent." Because I was so upset and something happened to my daughters or my mom or sisters. I was waiting for Ms. Naomi to come to the desk. I saw a lady walking through two double doors when, I looked down the hall. The sign read on the door. "Maternity Ward". I thought they had the wrong person. I thought to myself why am I waiting outside the maternity ward? She said really loud are you Ms. Gibson? I replied "yes" she had a baby wrapped in her arms. I looked at her and said who are you and who's baby is that? She said hers and she put the baby in my arms. I was very surprised and wondered if this was a mistake.

Matthew 18:10: Take heed that ye despise not one of these little ones; for I say unto you, that in heaven their angels do always behold the face of my Father which is in heaven.

14

I looked at the baby and she was so tiny. I was in shock and in my mind, I thought somebody is playing a joke on me. She asked me for my contact information, and you can take the baby home. I said wait a minute who's baby is this and why did you call me. She said your name was given as next of kin from Rosa. I said who is Rosa I don't know any Rosa, she said yes, she is your cousin. I started thinking I don't have a cousin name Rosa this is a bad mistake. She told me Rosa left the hospital and they are running around trying to find family to take the baby. By this time, the whole story was given to Ms. Naomi, the Social Worker at the hospital as I was family to this baby. I am still telling her I don't know this lady, nor do I have a cousin named Rosa. So, she said to me I know this is hard for you and I am sorry for calling you from your job. This can be a lot for one person. I began yelling saying this must be a mistake. How did you get my name and number she said your cousin Jane I said I don't have a cousin by that name she said, we spoke to her this morning she told me Ms. Gilbert could not take another baby? I stood there looking and thinking about how my name could been given to this Social Worker when I don't know any of these people who are supposed to be my cousins. I am looking at this beautiful little bundle of joy. My face and eyes swelled with tears. I said to the Social Worker what can I do to help you until you can straighten out this matter. She said we need to discharge the baby until we can locate her mother or other family members. Can you take the baby home with you? I stood there looking confused.

Lady, I said, and I work my daughters are at school I don't have a crib, baby clothes, or diapers. Who is going to watch the baby while I am working? She said, we will give you temporary foster care assistance. If you qualify to assist with childcare needs. I said the baby is a few days old and I would be very uncomfortable. I will contact my job to see if I can take emergency leave for two weeks until we can get things sorted out. The new bundle of joy was discharged in my care and they provided me with a car seat and some items until I was able to go shopping. I left the hospital to prepare my family on how I came to have a newborn baby since they saw me that morning. I arrived home to wait for the girls to get out of school. I contacted my mother to share with her what happened. I was on the phone with my mother and the little bundle of joy woke up and started to cry. My mother said who's baby is crying and I said that is why I was calling you. You won't believe what happen to me today. I told her how I got a phone call to come to the hospital and they gave me this baby. She is on the phone quiet. I said what do you think about it? My mother said are you sure that what happened I said mom yes. What are you thinking why you accepted a baby you don't know? What is the real issue? Did the mother of the child walk out the hospital and the police are looking for her?

My mother has told me she is coming over and I now hear my daughters coming in the door from school. They see the little bundle of joy wrapped in a blanket in my arms. They start smiling and asked who's baby is that? Is she staying with us, I replied to them yes, for a little a while and I inform them the mother of the baby is sick and they needed someone to look after her baby. The news traveled fast from my mother to my siblings. They came with questions about the baby. I explained the story of what happen at the hospital to my siblings. Of, course everyone was scratching their head about the new addition to the family. I was trying to get the house prepared for the little bundle of joy. My life changed in a matter of 13 hours as I went from 2 daughters to now having 3 daughters. I am home taking care of the little one still trying to figure how could someone give birth wake up and leave their child behind. I know that this woman must have a reason as to why, but God later revealed the story.

The little bundle of joy turned 2 months old and she is getting big and making noise. My mom agreed to keep her during the day while I'm at work. She found her way into our lives and we started bonding with her. My phone rings at work and it's Ms. Naomi. She asks me how things were going. She told me we would have to attend a court hearing. I am on the phone in shock. What do you mean we have to attend a court hearing? She explained to me, I will have to bring an attorney. I said why? There was something not done when I brought the little bundle of joy home from the hospital. She gave me the date to appear in court. I arranged to show up in court. I called around to look for an attorney; I was able to locate one who charged $250 an hour to represent me. I asked her many questions about what was going to happen in court. As she started gathering the facts of the case, I was told that the Social Services Agency did not follow proper protocol in giving me the little bundle of joy. I should have gone through a background check. My home should have gone through an inspection. None of these things happened as the attorney stated the caseworker was so rushed just to move on to other cases. Now I have to share this with my family. In the meantime, I took the new bundle to church one Sunday. The church members in the congregation coming up asking questions saying when did you have a baby, we didn't know you were pregnant. Who is the father? Some of the leadership in the church even was gossiping about me having about a new baby. I felt sad because the bible says in **Matthew 7:1**: Judge not, that ye be not judged. People are selfish when they think it is always important to know every situation of someone else affairs.

Preparing for the court hearing: The morning came to go to court and my attorney appeared and for the District and stated I was a stranger. In the courtroom the social service worker did not take the time to look for family members who may could take the little bundle of joy. My attorney stated that I was called as a family member to care for the baby. When I came to the hospital, I told the social worker I was not a family member. I was being blamed for errors made by the District. This was the beginning of more court trials. The Judge ordered for me to have a background check, psychological evaluation and for my daughters to be interviewed by a social worker. I stood up to the Judge and said? Your honor how is it I and being mistreated like a criminal and the mother of their baby abandoned her at the hospital. I was confused. You are asking information about my daughters. Is this the justice system or are you treating me this way because I am a single parent? The Judge looked at me and said talk to your attorney. I raised my voice again and said all due respect to your courtroom you are making these demands. He replied this is the order of the court and a date was set to return. My eyes swelled up with tears and I am saying to my attorney what just happened. She said let's step outside in the hallway. My attorney said the judge is trying to establish if there isn't any family to come forward you if you will be suitable for the baby to remain in your care. I replied and I said the baby has been with me for four months and no one came to my home or even called me. I said this is how little brown babies get treated in the system. He didn't ask how the baby was doing or what I think about the situation. The court assigned appointments to doctors, fingerprinting, background checks, and credit reporting of my financials. I had to supply my bank statements. I said to the attorney what if I changed my mind not to comply. She said I would be held in contempt of court and punishable to fines and possible jail. The attorney asked me if you are thinking of changing your mind let's start making decisions. I told her no I wouldn't change my mind even though this court system doesn't seem fair. If something happened to me, I would want someone to care for my daughters. The time it took to go through emotions of my children and my family. I worked two jobs because of the expense of legal fees, shelter, food and clothing for all 3 of my girls. My oldest is 13 years old, the middle 8 years old, and the bundle of joy. I served at my church as an assistant to the Bishop and I sat on the Trustee Board.

I was in a relationship at the time and this was not what he was looking to be involved in. I was hurt but I was okay because my life was full of working being a great mother and achieving advancement in my career. I was promoted on my job. I brought my first home. Now is the time to move and we are heading back to court for a statue hearing a year later the bundle is now 18 months old. The judge is being updated on the all the previous orders, while he listened to this information. The judge ordered whereabouts of the mother and father of the bundle. More things that should have been done is no fault of mine. This time I said nothing and I was very disappointed to see how our justice system worked. I told my attorney I want to adopt her and I am sure that this is what God has desired of me. She was so excited. The papers were filed. Two years later the court hearing was before another judge and the adoption was finalized. She was officially my daughter.

The parents were found by that time and the bundle of joy was by then 6 years old. The courts were going back to reverse the decision. The judge ruled that he will not rescind any order; the bundle is bonded in a loving family with a mother who sacrificed everything to ensure she has a bright future. That is my final ruling. She is happy, very spoiled, and loved by her sisters. The Lord will put us through an unexpected situation to show you he can work miracles in your life. When life gets hectic and you feel overwhelmed, take a moment to focus on the people and things you are most grateful for. When you have an attitude of gratitude, frustrating troubles will fall by the wayside. Just know that everything you need to accomplish your goals is already in you. Be gentle with yourself. You're doing the best you can! Always know Love cares, Love is selfless.

Authentic Strategies Notes

Name

Date

_____

_____

_____

_____

_____

_____

_____

_____

_____

_____

_____

_____

_____

Authentic Strategies Notes

Name

Date

_____

_____

_____

_____

_____

_____

_____

_____

_____

_____

_____

_____

Authentic Strategies Notes

Name

Date

_____

_____

_____

_____

_____

_____

_____

_____

_____

_____

_____

_____

Chapter 2

HEALTH FITNESS WELLNESS COACHES

New Life - chapter 2

BECOMING A HEALTHIER YOU – "THE TRANSFORMATION

Joi Brown

In life, there are birthdays that one can consider "milestones" such as 16, 21, 40, 50, etc. A milestone birthday can be considered a notable event that causes specific change to occur or that marks a specific point in the development of a person. With the countdown to my 40th birthday in 2019, I decided to make this birthday a special one to reflect a new season in my life. A season of new beginnings and possibilities and the need for me to become the best "Joi" I could be. I am Becoming a Healthier Me-The Transformation.

Transformation is considered a thorough or dramatic change in a form or appearance. Words such as change, alteration, modification, variation, amendments, evolution, remodeling, reshaping, redoing, reconstruction, rebuilding, reordering, revamping, reworking, and remaking are all words that I can attest as part of health and wellness journey.

From childhood to most of my adult life, I was overweight but active. I know, I know, you are thinking how can you be both be overweight and active? I was active in the sense of moving my body and doing some sort of physical activity like walking, dancing, or taking Zumba, spin, or cardio classes. You know being active can lead to numerus benefits from, reducing chronic diseases such as heart disease, cancer, diabetes, and stoke to improved sleep and self-confidence to relieving stress. Being active and exercising are steps to becoming healthier but without a change in my diet or portion sizes, I was still overweight and active.

I stand here as a living witness of my transformation, of losing over 100 pounds, that you can achieve anything you put your mind to if you do not give up. The journey was challenging at times, but so is life. There were good and bad days, just as life and days I did not feel like working out or wanting to eat the wrong foods. I did not stop; I persevered and kept going. If I can do it, so can you.

In life, we set goals for ourselves to achieve. For instance: wanting to lose 5 to 10 pounds, fitting into that black dress or favorite pair of jeans, reducing my daily medication or blood pressure, or learning to make healthier food choices are all realistic and attainable goals. It is never too late for a transformation and become the best version of yourself. I believe in you! Let me share some tips, strategies, and mindsets that helped me along my journey that I hope will help you with your transformation. Let's Get Ready To Transform!

1. Identify your "Why"

Identifying the why is key to your health and wellness goals. The why is the reason or purpose; think about why now are you deciding to make your health a priority? Writing down and posting your why is recommended and will serve as a reminder to you on those days when you want to throw in the towel.

My health journey began with my big sister asking me to join her and do Weight Watchers, and then later introducing me to a personal trainer, Keith Turner, who truly changed my life. At the time, my sister asked me if I was ready for a change, something new, so I decided to join. I remember being tired of how I looked, being active but still overweight. Enough was enough! I was ready and my why helped me achieve my goal. *Transformation Mindset--**Think About Why You Started.***

2. Identify your "How"

How are you going to include this fitness and healthier lifestyle into your day or week? With 24 hours a day, realistic thought of your schedule and time management is required to ensuring you make time for being active. Reviewing your schedule and identifying days and times that you can allocate time for physical activity is important. Seeking assistance or support from others is strongly encouraged.

I make time for what's important to me, working out and being active is part of my daily schedule. I have added workouts on my work schedule and most agencies allow time for health and wellness hours during the workweek. I cannot be there for others if I am unhealthy. *Transformation Mindset—**I love myself enough to work out daily.***

3. Do Workouts you Enjoy-you're more likely to stick with them

Find a physical activity you enjoy and commit to doing it. Do you like walking, water aerobics, bicycling, tennis, dancing, jogging, swimming, and gardening? There are numerous to choose from, the goal is to move. If you like swimming, then your perspective on swimming is different and you do not just view it as exercise.

My love for dance took me from dance attendee to instructor. As an instructor, I knew I wanted to help inspire and encourage women to be active and live their best life. Women who were like me, a mom, sister, daughter, or businesswomen understand that taking care of self is so important to fulfilling all the other roles in life. Transformation Mindset— **I love myself enough to work out daily.**

4. Start with a 30- Minute Workout

Commit to at least 30 minutes of working out or physical activity for three days until you can do it daily. Schedule it into your week like your nail, hair, or doctor's appointment. You are worth it so make the time. 30 minutes is a starting point if you cannot take a full hour class. The goal is to commit and start an activity that is more physical for at least 30 minutes for three to five days a week.

Starting my day off with a 30-minute walk has truly been rewarding to me. During my early morning walks, I have time to mediate and reflect on life or hear from God. Often times with the hustle and bustle of life, you miss hearing the birds chirp or seeing the trees change colors. When I walk, I am able to appreciate the activity of being able to move and enjoy what God has created around me. *Transformation Mindset—* **Be Focused. Be Persistent. Never Quit.**

5. Identify a Support System

Identifying your why is what motivated you to start but making things a habit is key to keeping up the longevity of the healthy lifestyle. Having friends, family, co-workers, and other fitness partners who understand the health and wellness journey will keep you committed and encouraged to reach your goals. Look at your inner circle and networks and identify your support system. Having a workout buddy or partner will keep you accountable on days when you don't feel like doing it and trying new workouts or activities. Go find your buddy!

I am truly grateful for my support system, which consist of my family, friends, Personal Trainer, Keith and his staff, and the other clients. From day one, I felt supported and encouraged during the workouts. Keith has pushed me beyond what I could have imagined for myself. It is truly a family affair, where we are one. *Transformation Mindset—* **Believe in Yourself. Believe You Can And Do It.**

6. Accept the Setbacks

Be patient with yourself. There will be good days and bad days and setbacks along the journey. If you thought this heath journey was super easy, NOT. There will be challenges. The key is to be persistent and keep going. Change is the only thing constant in life; prepare yourself to be the best version of yourself. You are becoming a healthier you. Don't be too hard on yourself and throw in the towel. If you have a setback it's for the day, not the week or month. Tomorrow is a new day to set new goals and achieve them. When setbacks occur, connect with your support system for encouragement or motivation. This is a healthy lifestyle not a diet that you are trying for a moment. Through the process, you will learn how to treat yourself and celebrate all what you have accomplished (e.g. remembering your why and goals) and know what to do when setbacks occur.

Along my journey, I have experienced many setbacks and felt upset and defeated. When I feel like that, I connect with my support system who provides a suggestion for me to try or gives me an encouraging word that will change my perception of the setback. I am often remembered for how far I have come and how I looked before I started and where I am today. My picture is a testament of the journey and I celebrate the milestone to reach the goal. In life, there are highs and lows, peaks and pits, when I have a setback I do not quit, and I push through. You can do this, push through. *Transformation Mindset—* **Visualize. You must see it, feel it, and experience it before it happens.**

7. Be You and Do You

Be you, do you, and do not compare yourself to others. Be willing to try new things. When you start, your jumping jacks, squats, sit-ups, etc. might not look like the class. It is okay, you are doing it and you will get better, keep trying. The goal is progress, not perfection. Remember everyone had a day one and were beginners. Find a workout atmosphere that is supportive and will make you accountable.

As a dance fitness instructor, you are often called to sub for other instructors. I had to learn that I can only be Joi, and my class was going to be different since I was not their instructor. I am a good instructor and if I bring my energy and personality to the class, it is going to be fun. I continue to make my own path and share my story of my health and weight loss journey with others. I want to inspire and encourage others to take care of our God given temple. *Transformation Mindset—**Clear your mind of Can't, You Can and Will.***

8. Small Steps Make Big Results

We live in a society where fast results and quick fixes have become the expectation. No pain, no gain is a foreign concept and the understanding that suffering or hard work is necessary to achieve something has been lost. Effective and long-lasting weight loss results require a lifetime commitment of exercise and healthy eating. Diets are short-term fixes, which restrict you from certain types of foods for a period. The weight you lost from the diet will come back if you go back to eating the food you gave up. Becoming a healthier you is about lifestyle changes that will help you achieve your why. What steps are you committed to doing as part of this process?

I can attest firsthand that hard work and consistency paid off. Just look at my picture, which shows my results. I started and got better with time and see how small steps made big results. This health journey is multi-faceted and heathy eating and exercise go together to create big results. *Transformation Mindset—* **Your hard work won't pay off overnight. Be Patient and you will see results a few months from now.**

9. Don't Eat It All

As a child, I learned to eat all the food on my plate and that food should not be wasted. Having no clear understanding that I should be eating until I am not hungry not until I am full or stuffed. Thanks to my trainer Keith, I understand and see how my eating till I am full contributed to me being overweight. Understanding the difference in portion and serving size is vital to knowing you don't have to eat it all. Portion size is how much food you choose to eat at one time, which may be more or less than a serving. Serving size is the amount of food listed on product's nutrition label. Portion size has increased, and adults are eating more and consuming more calories contributing to American being obese. It is not too late to become a healthier you. You have to start.

I have learned to make healthier food choices in terms of serving size and portion size. I have identified health snacks and new recipes to create new healthier dishes. After a rigorous workout, if I eat the wrong foods or eat until I am stuffed, the workout I just did was for nothing. Using measuring cups and spoons as guide to assist me make sure my portion and serving size is the same is a great tip. There are numerous tools from American Heart Association and U.S. Department of Agriculture to aid you on creating healthy plate. *Transformation Mindset*— **Being healthy is 30% working out (exercise) and 70% diet (what you eat).**

10. Accountable

Accountability is key to reaching your health goals. Weight loss programs are more effective and successful if there is an accountability measure. What gets measured is done is a motto I live by. Weekly weigh-ins are my accountability measure by my trainer Keith holds my process and me accountable to losing weight is measured through weekly weigh-ins. What I eat and following his meal plans will determine if I achieve the goal of losing weight for that week.

Being held accountable also helps me stay focused and motivates me to achieve results. Remember, your support system is there to keep you accountable as well; you are not in this alone. When you feel like that cake or cookie is calling you, use your support system as your lifeline. The support system is a great resource to help you overcome challenges and setbacks and will keep you accountable. *Transformation Mindset*— *Fitness is like a marriage; you can't cheat on it and expect it to work.*

I have been transformed and continue to evolve into becoming the best Joi I can be in all areas of my life. I believe in you; you can do it! I hope my tips, strategies, and mindsets will inspire you to join this journey with me and Become a Healthier You - The Transformation.

Transformation questions to assist you on your journey:

1. What is your why for becoming a healthier you?
2. What barriers are impending you from achieving your why?
3. What physical activities do you like doing?
4. How can you incorporate physical activity into your life?
5. Who in your support system?
6. What does success look like?
7. How will you hold yourself accountable?

THE HEARTBEAT OF WATER

Charlene Harrod-Owuamana

Let's get relaxed and enjoy this moment with Water, Music and Mediation.

Did you know that water has a HEARTBEAT? It flows to a specific rhythm. Depending on the elements it flows over - it makes marvelous music. Water is used for agriculture, industry and electricity.

Water...

Allows the body to absorb and assimilate minerals, vitamins, amino acids, glucose and other substances. It flushes toxins and waste products from the body. Helps regulate temperature. It also acts as a lubricant for joints and muscles.

BENEFITS OF WATER

A certain amount of water is necessary for our daily task and purposes in life. Most states, countries and governments use water differently. In addition, their benefits are different as well, here are a few:

- domestic and mutual use
- Industrial use
- Irrigation
- Mining
- Hydroelectric power
- Navigation
- Recreation
- Public Parks
- Wildlife

OUR SURVIVAL WITH WATER

We all use water for drinking, washing, cleaning, cooking, and growing food. It adds to our daily routines at home. It generates electricity, used in manufacturing products and transporting goods and services. This is an excellent segway to talk about conserving water and having safe drinking water.

The average person uses more than 300 gallons of water at home daily, according to the United States Environmental Protection Agency (EPA). It seems like a very high number but let's think about how we use water in our daily lives. Whether we are home or out of the house. Most of the WATER we use comes from local lakes, rivers, streams, or underground aquifers, depending on your city/state and/or country.

We also use water for other resources such as:

- Watering lawns, flowers, gardening, washing cars, filling swimming pools, etc.

We need to be mindful of the chemicals we use and how we dispose of those chemicals and other elements.

"If we paid attention to the amount of water, we use daily. We might be able to understand why it cost so much and, why our bills continue to rise. Local, State and other countries and jurisdiction need to pay close attention on being sure the water sources are clean and available."

MAKING MUSIC WITH WATER

"Who would have thought that water makes its own music ?" 🎵

Listen to a flow of water when reading this Chapter. You will experience a new you. Begin to meditate daily while listening to the flow of water. Cleanse your soul. Cleanse your mind. Cleanse who you are and who you will become. While writing this chapter and any articles, and books, I have found a new way to get into myself. It is by SOUNDS, not taste, not touch and not by feeling. Although we experience different feels with WATER.

IT HAS AMAZED ME - How water plays several important roles in our lives.

Spiritual * Physical * Mental

RELAXATION

You do not need to be by the water to experience this NEW Beginning. There are several different items, sources and elements one can use to create their own experiences. Take a moment while reading this chapter to reflect on creating a "Water Heartbeat". I will leave a mini journal at the end of my chapter to inspire you to create your very own. It won't cost a lot, just take your time and create an OASIS.

LET TALK ABOUT WHAT WATER IS USED FOR.... {Can be used for direct & indirect purposes}

DIRECT PURPOSE

Drinking - Needing daily source of clean water to nourish our bodies.

Cooking - Needing daily sources of clean water to prepare of food.

Bathing - Needing daily sources of clean water to cleanse our bodies.

Blessing - Needing spiritual guidance to cleanse our souls.

INDIRECT PURPOSE

Processing wood to make paper and producing steel for automobiles. Who would have thought that water was used for these items?

15 % of water is consumed daily by:

- Drinking
- Bathing
- Cooking
- Washing Dishes
- Washing Clothes
- Cleaning fruits/vegetables
- Brushing Teeth. And the list goes on...

SPIRITUAL WATERS

Water is the last step before increase. Water helps things to grow. If you nurture things, items and seeds - that have been planted. You will have a greater harvest.

1 Corinthians 3:3-5

3 You are still worldly. For since there is jealousy and quarreling (<u>A</u>) among you, are you not worldly? Are you not acting like mere humans? **4** For when one says, "I follow Paul," and another, "I follow Apollos," (<u>B</u>) are you not mere human beings?

5 What, after all, is Apollos? (<u>C</u>) And what is Paul? Only servants, (<u>D</u>) through whom you came to believe—as the Lord has assigned to each his task.

God's will for increase in your life. Take the information and do what you need. Faith without water; you will not have growth. Let's talk about the seed and water. You must know how to water the seed. Watering is the transition point from what you will see after your harvest. Have you ever been watered? Understanding watering is common and the seed will grow. Let's talk about how a seed grows. As it relates to our life:

1. Our life being the container
2. We must feed our bodies nourishments
3. Hydrate our bodies with water
4. Exercise
5. Hydrate our bodies with water
6. Continue our daily task
7. Hydrate our bodies with water
8. Eliminate
9. Hydrate our bodies with water
10. Outdoor activities
11. Hydrate our bodies with water
12. Bathe
13. Hydrate our bodies with water

Water is essential for your spiritual upkeep of your body. It helps with clarity, preparation and body movements.

We have been planted. Let's talk about the seed we were planted from...

When you were in the womb, you were surrounded by fluids or water. You were able to survive during your growth period. The fluids surrounding you had to be at a certain level in order to sustain life.

MY CRY

My tears have a distinct taste. Tears are made up of three components:

1. Lipids (oil)
2. Water
3. Mucus

Each component serves its own purpose. The outside component is the oil - it smooths the surface and keeps it from drying out. The watery layer is in the middle - makes up what you see the most. It washes away foreign particles and cleans the eye. The mucus layer is the inner layer, and its purpose is to spread the watery layer over the eye surface to keep it moist. Tears keeps the eyes healthy and comfortable.

WATERFALLS

Waterfalls often relate to a great release of emotion, rejuvenation, and renewal of spirit. It represents openness, flexibility, power, form, and spirituality, which is an ancient symbol association with water in its myriad manifestations. There are many different religions that symbolize waterfalls and here are two examples:

In Islam, the waterfall symbol can mean focus on an important decision, but the focus needs to be clear.

In the Christian tradition, a waterfall can symbolize the insistence of intentions, exceptional career luck, and an invitation to delight the observer.

Blessed oil Vs. Blessed water

Oil symbolizes God's mercy and when used in anointing it is a visible embodiment of the grace of healing. Christians, therefore, often keep small bottles of holy oil in their icon corner and anoint themselves and others of their family with the sign of the Cross in holy oil. This anointing is usually done on the individual's forehead and is used for the same reasons for which holy water is used.

Holy water may be used in cases where a person falls under the power of evil spirits. The individual should be encouraged to drink some of the sanctified water and be sprinkled with it. At times when members of the family feel an especially evil force within the home, the head of the family should sprinkle the inside walls of the family church with holy water in the same manner as is done by the priest.

It depends on the nature of the issues, whether holy oil or holy water will be used. As long as, it is used in the proper manner; then the outcome will be for the greater outcome. Knowing when, where and how to utilize the holy oil and/or holy water. They both should be applied by:

The priest or the bishop must bless the oil.

- Blessed hands.
- In the shape of a cross on the forehead.
- Each represents a different cause.

SONGS ABOUT WATERFALLS

When you feel down, depressed, hopeless and/or irritable. Then, turn on music and sit in a quiet place and listen to the words and/or the instruments used. One can find this has been soothing to the mind & heart. This can help you spiritually, physically and emotionally. Here is a list of sons about Waterfalls and Springs.

➤ Waterfalls by TLC
➤ Waterfalls by Paul McCartney
➤ Waterfall by Wendy & Lisa
➤ Waterfalls by Lakeview
➤ Every Teardrop is a Waterfall by Coldplay
➤ Waterfall by Stone Roses
➤ Waterfall by Gavin DeGraw
➤ Splash Waterfalls by Ludacris
➤ Waterfall by 10cc
➤ By a Waterfall by Guy Lombardo
➤ Waterfall by Electric Light Orchestra
➤ Eyes Waterfalling by Level 42
➤ Over the Waterfall by Michelle Shocked
➤ May This Be Love (aka Waterfall) by Jimi Hendrix
➤ Waterfall by Carly Simon

- ➤ Springs of Life by Ginny Owens
- ➤ Silver Waterfalls by Siouxsie & The Banshees
- ➤ Waterfall by Peter Frampton
- ➤ Run Down the Waterfall by The Promise Ring
- ➤ Singing Waterfall by Hank Williams
- ➤ Nature Springs by The Good, The Bad and The Queen
- ➤ Waterfall by The Toadies
- ➤ Dance On a Waterfall by Orange Blue
- ➤ Love Song of a Waterfall by Slim Whitman
- ➤ Waterfall by Bananaram

To summarize this chapter...

Water is general, productive of public benefit, which promotes peace, health, safety and welfare of the STATE. WATER is beneficial for our lives. To nourish our bodies and provide protection. Conserving water is important - because water sometimes does not return to its original location and sometimes is not the same quality and/or quantity. Failing to conserve water can lead to lack of adequate, healthy water supply and more drastic consequences in rising cost, reduced food surpluses, health hazards and political conflict. Listening to music can help soothe the soul and take your mind off any problems. This is known as "Music Therapy". Music Therapy is the clinical and evidence-based use of music interventions to accomplish individualized goals. It addresses physical, emotional, cognitive, and social needs of individuals. After listening to one or two of the songs above, share your thoughts below:

_____

_____

_____

_____

_____

_____

_____

Thank you for your support on "THE HEARTBEAT OF WATER". TAKE THIS TIME TO RELECT ON YOUR CLOSENESS WITH WATER! And enjoy this; 3 DAY * Journal and

Affirmation....

THE HEARTBEAT OF WATER - 3 DAY Journal and Affirmation....

Do this activity while listening to the flow of water, come back to this chapter a week later and read your answers aloud to yourself.

DAY 1

John 7:38 - He that believeth on me, as the scripture hath said, out of his belly shall flow rivers of living water.

Affirmation: I AM: _____

Bible Verse: _____

Daily Goals:

_____

_____

_____

_____

_____

DAY 2

Isaiah 49:10 - They shall not hunger nor thirst; shall neither the heat nor sun smite them: for he that hath mercy on them shall lead them, even by the springs of water shall he guide them.

Affirmation: I AM: _____

Bible Verse: _____

Daily Goals:

_____

_____

_____

_____

_____

DAY 3

Proverbs 5:15 - Drink waters out of thine own cistern and running waters out of thine own well.

Affirmation: I AM: _____

Bible Verse: _____

Daily Goals:

_____

_____

_____

_____

_____

Take a picture reading my Chapter "THE HEATBEAT OF WATER" and post on my social media page.

FACEBOOK: Charlene Harrod-Owuamana

Health and Fitness

Milagros Richards

I will not give you a recipe or a workout formula; I am just going to break up this term and how to use it to improve your daily living. Most of us know that we need at least 30 minutes of a workout routine at least 3 days a week. We also know that we need to eat a balanced, healthy diet to stay fit and healthy. Sleep at least seven hours a day to have a logical mind and a more productive day.

So, what are health and fitness according to the internet? "Health is the level of functional or metabolic efficiency of a living organism. In humans, it is the ability of individuals or communities to adapt and self-manage when facing physical, mental, or social challenges…health is a state of complete physical, mental and social well-being and is not merely the absence of disease or infirmity" (World Health Organization, 1946).

Nowadays in the world where everything seems to change daily, being healthy and physically fit is a challenge. We restrict health in our vocabulary to eating right and exercising, but you need both mental and physical health. Health is in everything that we do in our daily life anything from the way you feel, your quality of life, the focus you have at work, your ability to move, your psychological state, and the way we interact with family and friends. The way people treat us, the way we perceive people, assuming things in our own way, which is not healthy at times. Communication is a very important part of a healthy relationship, also has a state of mind where your mental health is in shape. Mental health is important because it will affect our physical health, so if we stay mentally healthy, we will be physically healthy even in times of despair.

Fitness is described as going out to the gym and exercising, different from what you will see in a dictionary or what health experts will say, fitness is not only physical but it's also mental and fitness could be how we treat others and how we treat ourselves. The words health and fitness are usually combined in a sentence because they go hand-in-hand; practicing them together, they can make us whole and will help us realize our potential in many ways. At least 30 minutes of exercise per day will help you release endorphins that will make a person happy and magnanimous; making new friends and feel good about oneself and others. Eating healthy will help you with your overall health and body functions. My favorite quote: "Those who bear the weight will wear the crown! What type of crown are you trying to wear? Wealth, fame, health, or love!" Author unknown.

Authentic Strategies Notes

Name

Date

_____

_____

_____

_____

_____

_____

_____

_____

_____

_____

_____

_____

Authentic Strategies Notes

Name

Date

_____

_____

_____

_____

_____

_____

_____

_____

_____

_____

_____

_____

_____

_____

Authentic Strategies Notes

Name

Date

_____

_____

_____

_____

_____

_____

_____

_____

_____

_____

_____

_____

Chapter 3

PROFESSIONAL
DEVELOPMENT

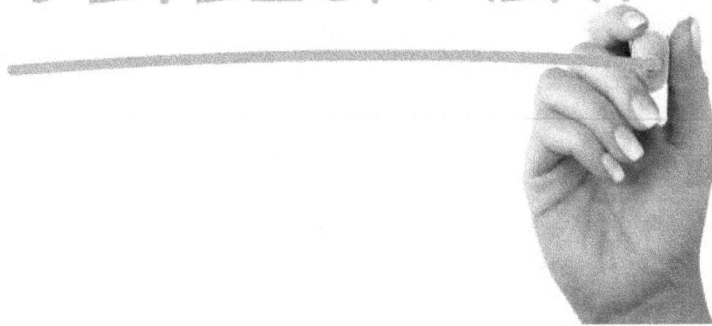

Beware of Coaching Hustlers!

By Dr. Jennifer Jones Bryant

Working as a certified life coach and career strategist for several years, I have learned from personal experience and observed the destructive behaviors made within the coaching industry. These behaviors give clients a wrong perception and can turn them away from the industry altogether. My chapter will focus on defining coaching; identifying coaching hustler's destructive behaviors, providing additional tips so clients can do their due diligence before hiring a certified coach, and adding best practices in a coach's toolkit.

What is Coaching?

Definitions of professional coaching include:

- **School of Coaching Mastery definition of coaching**: Coaching is a customized conversation that leads to personal growth and empowers the client to get what s/he wants by thinking and acting more resourcefully.
- **International Coach Federation (ICF) definition of coaching**: Coaching is partnering with clients in a thought-provoking and creative process that inspires them to maximize their personal and professional potential (Best Practices for Professional Coaches, https://www.schoolofcoachingmastery.com)

Let the Buyer Beware!

Watch out for those coaches who do not have their credentials. Because the coaching industry is unregulated, some wake up one morning and self-designate themselves as coaches. While some may be well meaning, they do not have the requisite training and operate on false beliefs and methods to leave a client harmed.

Ten inappropriate coaches' behavior you should be aware of before hiring a coach:

1. Making assumptions about the circumstances of a client's life: without fully understanding the big picture is a critical coaching mistake. Additionally, making assumptions about a client's beliefs, feelings, perspectives, values, strengths, and weaknesses, and their thought process can affect a coaching session's progress. A life coach needs to have a comprehensive understanding of a client's behavior before any concrete conclusions about a client's psychological tendencies can be reached.

2. Not actively listening intently to a client's verbal and non-verbal communication: If a life coach is not mirroring and repeating what they heard the client say, they may not have a complete understanding of their client's perspective. Repeating what you heard from the client allows them to correct misunderstandings or any assumptions that the life coach may be making.

3. Not asking powerful questions for the client to have self-discovery: At all times, a life coach must remain neutral on all issues and should use the power of asking powerful questions and observing verbal and nonverbal cues. If they find they cannot do this with a particular client, they should stop coaching them immediately. If a life coach isn't asking insightful, open-ended, and reflective questions, their questions are only not going to assist their client with making the changes they desire to realize. The more insightful the question, the more thought is required, and the more likely the client will be able to find a suitable answer and have self-discovery.

4. **Coaches who try to serve as a therapist:** when a client is dealing with mental illness, divorce, or sexual assaults, or other major life traumatic events, the coach should uphold ethics and refer them to psychologists and psychiatrists trained in this area.

5. **Confusing Coaching vs. Mentoring:** It is vital not to bring your personal experiences and perspective in a coaching discussion because it does not allow the client to problem solve, and if your unsolicited "advice" does not work, the coach can be blamed. Assuming a mentor relationship when a client wants a coach may have long-term effects and delays on the client's continued growth and development.

6. **Promising Results:** Some coaches play on client's vulnerabilities and make promises instead of working in partnership with the client for the desired outcome. The coach

serves as an accountability partner while the client achieves their goals and desired outcomes. Professional coaches never should put profits above client results.

7. **Breaking Confidentiality:** Coaches should design an alliance with their client to ensure a strong foundation of how you will work together as a team. A designed alliance is an agreement between the coach and client; therefore, the life coach must not discuss the client's circumstances with anybody else, unless the client threatens to cause harm to themselves or others.

8. **Investing Emotions in Your Client:** Coaches must leave their emotions and oversharing their personal problems during the sessions because it will not yield positive results. It is essential to remain professional and neutral. Most importantly, coaches should take care of their mental, physical, and emotional wellbeing. If needed, coaches should cancel sessions when they are not up to the appointment with their clients.

9. **Not Allowing the Client to Initiate Topics for Discussion:** Not allowing the client to initiate the agenda could lead to unpredictable consequences that may push a client away from coaching or lead them down an undesirable path. If the client follows your agenda, they will be following your plan instead of their own.

10. **Professional coaches should neither sell nor upsell during coaching sessions:** Coaches should schedule separate conversations to discuss additional products or services that the client may want, and they are transparent about the nature of those conversations. Life coaches use marketing tools such as email, social networking sites, tele classes, webinars, live networking, etc., to build relationships with people. The focus should not be on squeezing profits from prospective clients. Building relationships and rapport attracts clients and leads to coaching success, while the latter erodes trust. Professional coaches fully inform their clients about the services and fees to expect from coaching, before paid coaching commences, and they take care to deliver what they promise.

This list is not all encompassing and will assist with a client's research when they hire a certified coach.

According to the ICF How to Select a Coach, here are some questions you may want to ask prospective coaches (https://icf-cle.clubexpresscom) before hiring:

1. What is your coaching experience? (Number of individuals coaches, years of experience, types of situations)
2. What is your coach-specific training? Do you hold an ICF Credential, or are you enrolled in an Accredited Training Program?
3. What are your coaching specialties or client areas you most often work?
4. What specialized skills or experience do you bring to your coaching?
5. What is your philosophy about coaching?
6. What is your specific process for coaching? (How sessions are conducted, frequency, etc.)
7. What are some coaching success stories? (Specific examples of individuals who have been helped through your coaching).

The additional tips will be helpful as the prospective client hires a coach:

1. Please do your homework and educate yourself about what coaching is, what it is not, and what the coaching process entails.
2. Reflect on your goals and objectives.
3. Interview at least three coaches.
4. Confirm credibility through past testimonies; research them through google, and social media.
5. Get written coaching agreements that describe in detail what the client can expect and include a link to the ethical code or best practices to which the coach adheres.

As with every profession, life coaching brings a delicate balance of techniques, strategies, and tools that, when used correctly, can bring about positive change within people. However, when misused or rather abused, these tools can affect a client's livelihood in very unpredictable ways. As life coaches, we have a responsibility to protect our client's best interests at all times. We must be very vigilant of our every word, behavior, and action to ensure that it is consistent with the intent of meeting our client's needs now and in the future.

A productive and meaningful partnership with a certified coach is rewarding for your self-discovery and goal achievement after following the above steps and tips. Every day, I hold myself accountable for upholding my life coaching certification and providing my clients with the best experience by adhering to tips, industry best practices, and focusing on my purpose. I strive to deliver my best to my clients by helping them to reach within, ignite their fire to realize their potential and passion.

Authentic Strategies Notes

Name

Date

_____

_____

_____

_____

_____

_____

_____

_____

_____

_____

_____

_____

_____

_____

Authentic Strategies Notes

Name

Date

_____

_____

_____

_____

_____

_____

_____

_____

_____

_____

_____

_____

Authentic Strategies Notes

Name

Date

_____

_____

_____

_____

_____

_____

_____

_____

_____

_____

_____

_____

_____

Chapter 4

Personal Development Rocks

Speak Life into HerStory

Reactivate and Value your Vision Goddess
Shawna Halley

As your premier ambassador for women's authentic living, let's keep it real right from the start…

***Moment of truth*----*Do you sometimes feel held back by feelings of uncertainty and discomfort?* This is especially prevalent among aspiring women leaders** who oftentimes doubt their abilities and over-think, over-analyze, or over-process the idea of just getting started and living full out. In fact, many drop their dreams due to distraction and fear. Does this sound familiar to you?

How much longer will you allow yourself to be afflicted and poisoned by the past? I understand stepping into the world to show up, as an 'Unstoppable Visionary Woman' requires massive COURAGE! After all, 'WE/women' are the future to restoring a thriving global community, so we must get to work to leave that positive legacy. 'Be Legends, not ladies.' This path is often permeated with fears, risks, uncertainty, challenges, and setbacks that make it appear less than favorable when considering launching into our divine purpose with passion to profit.

I once met a woman who felt alone and ashamed of her past. Her story in her eyes was too much to share; even the thought of it was like a block of cement she carried daily. I asked her to share bit-by-bit. Like a withered rose she began to bloom again. **Her inner sanctuary** that was once cluttered and corroded with self-hate began to sparkle like the sun after refreshing rain. She made the decision to release old trauma and drama and reclaim peace, happiness, and clarity. These are the gifts of a centered life.

"Who are you to be successful?" - Voice of the inner critic compels!

What is your answer to this invisible critic-imposter, poverty princess who dares to question your right to succeed? Your right to live like a Goddess. Your right to line up with your purpose, prosperity, divinity, and destiny unapologetically!

Imagine responding to this phony, who was implanted into your psyche way back when...with these jaw dropping words..._**Silhouettes of Strategies from the real you, Visionary Divine Woman who seeks to focus forward, speak her TRUTH!**

"As I sat and watched the setting sun, relief and joy of a new day begun.

I gave up denial, I gave up hurt,

 I gave up what I thought was a future covert.

My mind now focused on the will to be FREE. The self-imprisonment key was released.

I glanced once more at my gaping past and turned to focus on what I willed for my new path."- "Shawna Halley"

Did you know an ironing board is a surfboard that gave up on her dreams? Rise Woman Awaken to your Inner Wonder; come alive, live free, reconnect to your destiny (Goddess Identity), think like a leader, grow!

I remember the first time when I realized that my mission and purpose was to serve women. To show them the way out of a life filled with duty driven thinking and actions. It was after I invested in my first official partnership business. You see I had several small businesses, at this point I decided to go big. I was afraid until I felt the first spark, the inspiration to improve the health and economic conditions of women by supporting them as they transition, transcend, and transform their minds to identify with their Divine Goddess nature. The partnership failed, I had given up my day job, went all in with every dollar I had save. Within a month, it was all gone. Depression and suicidal thoughts set in. Isolation became my best friend, as I ruminate on feeling ashamed and guilty for not stopping when I saw the signs. It was all gone now. But God my Source reminded of the promise "I will never leave nor forsake you." It was not a dead end, just a detour. "Be of good cheer, I will be with you till the end."

As I laid one night feeling sorry for myself a show came on PBS by Dr. Wayne Dyer "I can See Clearly Now" followed by "You Can Heal your Life" by Louise Hay. Through these series of events, just to keep the story short, I was introduced to my life coach who took me through a process that transformed my life. This became the second spark on how I was meant to serve, uplift, and transform women's lives. I receive epiphanies often on how to serve on a larger scale and I said YES to my purpose by valuing my vision. How by trusting the transformation process and having faith filled actions to keep me growing and contributing to women's right to show up and speak up authentically without feeling like an imposter.

My greatest gift to you is to remember who you are and that this is your time to value your vision by sharing your gifts with the world. Take off the basket and let your light shine. An 'Unstoppable Visionary Woman' knows she is always three feet from her next pot of gold. **Gold of NEW solutions; Gold NEW of ideas; Gold of NEW adventure; Gold of NEW resources and prosperity all waiting for her to claim**. Remember the promise, "He said all your hairs are numbered, you are more than a sparrow that falls. He said I came that you might have life that's why I placed my kingdom inside you. I asked you to be the essence of love. I came that you may live abundantly, and stop settling for pennies and meager fees. Just like King Solomon accept your inner and outer treasures, this is wisdom and wealth. Let your light shine, think Big, a woman who deserves compensation for her service in exchange. Time to show up, stand up, and speak out. Delivery of your gift is tied to some one's liberation and freedom. Don't die full, die empty and give it all you've got."

Imagine you give yourself permission to KNOW for Sure…

- You belong at the table; the vision is for you to create a business you would be proud to work in.
- You are the **Passport**, you will **Passionately** step into your **Purpose**, and you are ready to **Prosper** and **Profit**.
- **You can lead your life** and generate long term satisfaction all on your terms? Opportunity knocks!!!

WHY???

"A woman who knows her worth.

Is like a golden nugget; that never loses its luster.

A woman who is guided from WITHIN.

Is like a lighthouse you can trust to show you the way to --Honor the Goddess Within.

A woman who needs no outer approval to feel joy.

Is like a rose that blooms every hour on the hour.

A woman who shares her LOVE.

Is like the Universe saying, I know and accept that we are ONE.

A woman who is satisfied with her life.

Is like a magnet that draws to it Love, beauty, simplicity, light, and clarity in every moment.

YOU are that woman-embrace the truth of who you are in this very hour."

Now is the Time to Awakening Goddess! Now is the time to set yourself FREE! Now is the time, RISE woman makes it an emergency!

Self-Reflection to Self-Evolution

Silhouettes of Strategies:

Power of asking the right questions as well as giving lucid clear answers, will narrow your results and accelerate ideas for solutions. Answer the following questions; remember rapid solution-oriented results are based on the clarity of your questions & answers.

Speak up Goddess

1. What is your plan?
2. Is your ship sailing without the captain?
3. What is the destination?
4. Why go there anyway?
5. How bad do you want it?
6. Is it seared on your subconscious; I'm talking about your vision?
7. Who will serve those you were meant to liberate?

Speak up; give yourself permission to sparkle Goddess.

Expect to Lead

Speak up about your message; it can change someone's life.

Know your part, play your role, you are the leading lady, don't be a tag along in your own life.

Learn five ways to deliver when you're in the spotlight.

Time to 'Speak up' your voice and words are like music to someone's ear and nourishment to their bones. So, 'Stand Out & Speak Up.'

Imagine you are the most powerful force in the universe. How, so glad you ask. Here are three reasons you need to value your vision, making you an 'Unstoppable Visionary Woman'. These are three of the most powerful forces in your universe

1. The human soul on fire with desire
2. A life on purpose
3. A Woman who values and pursues her vision relentlessly

You are the **R**eturn **O**n your **I**nvestment. Listen to the Chinese proverb that says,

"The best time to plant a tree is 20 years ago; the next best time is NOW today."

4-Signs you are not valuing your vision

▶ Constantly feel like an imposter.
▶ Find yourself wondering if you are in the right place.
▶ With the right person.
▶ Worse completely wrong century or lifetime?

ARE you READY to Value your vision then ...?

✓ **Choose** your Goddess Identity-Greater is he who is in me…so I must be a Goddess.
✓ **Choose** prosperity- I came that you might have life, life abundantly.
✓ **Choose** your inheritance- it is yours by birthright- No one can fill your shoes- all of your hairs are numbered you are greater than a sparrow that falls.
✓ **Choose** to shine your light, so that those that need you can see you clearly. Stop hiding-permission granted you are FREE to deliver your gifts to the world.
✓ **Choose** to let go of the imposter cloak get into the dream chamber and write your vision down.

Speak up Goddess...

- Do you want to transform lives and share your message with the world?
- Are you READY to find your voice, share your message and change thousands of lives in the next 90 days?
- Would you like to be paid for your advice, serve from your heart and with magical miracle producing passion?
- Would you like to learn how to create a powerful presentation to move your audience from inaction to massive action in under 24 hours? I can show you how.

My Mission an Invitation

"Guidance from Spirit and the Universe.

Thought by thought, we happily traverse.

Step by step we joyfully look ahead, before we know it, we're living the

dream, vision seen.

Come walk with me, let's make this journey a breeze.

Life has highs and lows

Let's Consciously Create more HIGHS than lows."-Shawna Halley

I serve the woman behind the business; she is a leader and wearing the CEO hat. Whether she is single, single mom, or divorced, this is my area of expertise. I was a young mother of 4 by age 25, divorced, single parent, experience being homeless all by age 35. Still I RISE amid it all. Owned two homes; obtained several degrees and certifications; a flourishing career and much more!

Detour is not denial. Ask yourself when a problem arise, Is it an obstacle, or an opportunity? Perspective is everything.

Thank you for sharing this time with me. See you at the top, top of your game. Serving with your unique Divine Goddess Gifts.

Your Next step: https://www.prismoftransformation.com/introductory-offer

Or Schedule:

Invitation to a FREE Conscious Life Exploration Session
https://app.acuityscheduling.com/schedule.php?owner=19976704

www.prismoftransformation.com

Self-Love

Overcoming to Elevate

Victoria Holland

What does it really mean to overcome? What does it really require overcoming? Will overcoming last? These are just so mere questions that we may ask ourselves because of the process releasing the very thing that causes the pain. Yes, pain and overcoming it are associated the question is what we do first. Through this thing called "my life", I learned that in most cases I became the very person holding me back from pursing the very thing I wanted. To be me in the mist of everything required going through the very steps that I would later teach others in my classes.

The first piece of overcoming was understanding the definition and looking at it from a different perspective. So, what is the overcoming? So glad you have begun to understand the process of probing questioning. There are so many definitions to this little word but when I put it to use for me it was simple to put together my own. Overcoming to me is the successful awareness that I have mastered going past something that I thought was unattainable for me. We often want to fit into the puzzle just perfectly when in most cases we cannot or do not. We must journey past that what is expected. Everything must come with realizing that you must go beyond just succeeding over it but mastering going past.

When I was much younger, I was told I would never be able to read effectively because I talked too much. How hilarious was that because the very thing that was told to me would hinder me would be the very thing that would help me go past mastering reading. The very thing that you see is a problem we must learn to use to our advantage as a tool to help successfully to going past the very thing that would hold you from moving. When we began to see that the bad is truly working towards our good. One of the things that has become very apparent the bible speaks so very clearly of the things that will move us past that which is considered a problem. With everything, there is a season and a purpose and that speaks of going PAST to succeed that is Overcoming.

With anything, the first thing to address the "it" is that you want to overcome. For me it was overcoming myself realizing that I was standing in my own way and that my blessings and those that God had assigned to me was being held up in my pain. The pain of my past, the present and even possibly the future. What did I need to do to get past "this"! I had to come up with a plan that would force me to go past what I was looking at the hurt. I had to develop something that would give me the energy back into my life that no one even realized was gone I had to Overcome ME. The plan required me to address the root of the problem. The plan required that I do something that was different from before. Have you had similar conversations with yourself, but you realize that your problem when you became transparent that you did not know how to determine what the different should be? Through developing the plan, it fails on my spirit that God had the ultimate suggestion if you. Writing the Vision and Making It Plain.

This came to me so clearly that it took me back to those days back in the early 90's when I worked with the Area Agency on Aging when I wrote the first grant proposal that had ever been written for that particular agency. It was something that I had never done before in my life but became so rewarding in that it took me out of my comfort zone of business. Excellent idea God! Let me use that same process to develop a plan for me to Overcome Me! As I began, I realize that I was addressing the issue and then the plan. My attitude automatically turned upside down and backwards until I could laugh. This is now a group workshop that I teach "Adjusting Your Upside A." When you are moving towards Elevating to something positive, we must adjust the attitude that we have towards it.

At that very moment when God reminded me of that process was when I realize that I was on the road to Overcoming. I was at that very moment moving towards Overcoming to Elevate through identifying the problem, taking ownership for it, adjusting my Attitude and now devising a working plan that would force me to grow. If there is no growth, there is very little Elevation. Can you just imagine remaining in an infant mindset at the age of 57? God clearly identifies this when He stated that when "when I was a child, I acted like a child but when I became an adult, I put away childish things." This is the very thing that right now continues to confuse me with some. We all have issues, and we all have things that we need assistance in adjusting but we continue to have childlike behavior. Where is the growth potential?

After I realize that I was moving toward overcoming, I began to put the plan in action. The first as for stated the attitude adjusting, so what was next? Again, another probing question. Evaluating my history with processing some of the issues that caused the previous result.

Well that was somewhat easy as I sit here laughing aloud; it was the players in my mental drama play. Often times we play the main character in our own production but what about those supporting actors, keep in mind sometimes those individuals are in our head as well as in the natural the key is identifying their roles and placing them where they belong. If you are going to overcome, then evaluating the pieces in our history and if they are currently necessary. That was the part for me that was easy removing people, places, and things that did not add value. I am sure you are asking how or even why. Simply put, I was sick as you should be of going around and around in the same circle and feeling drained. That was not the feeling I wanted or needed. I needed Elevation and in order to get there I had to Overcome the connections. We must understand that this can be hard if we are not ready be alone at times, however; the prize of peace will be worth it.

One of the next parts of Overcoming to Elevate is that of creating new innovative ways to move you forward. I developed a whole Re-dedication process for myself that held me accountable as I evaluate how much I respected myself, loved myself and found the real value of myself. I know often times we as Coaches encourage individuals to have accountability partners but as usual, I never have done anything like anyone else even in this industry. I honestly believe we have to set the Overcoming to Elevate bar high. That comes from holding ourselves accountable first! I have had partners but sometimes they were not available, and I had to tackle the task at hand on my own. The question I had to say to myself was 'How bad did I really want it this time?' The answer was yet again stronger, after completing all of the nine steps that I created for myself that I now teach (I only shared a few here). I was able to see what I had overcome and that when I looked into my mental and physical mirror I realize that I was over so many struggles in my life that left space of peace.

Another key in Overcoming to Elevate is the price that we have put on ourselves. Why is that important? Because we have continued to be devalued by society and sometimes, that has even caused us to devalue ourselves. We have been programmed for so long that we have to measure up when in fact that is incorrect. In one of my recent classes one of my students determined that her value was not based on who she was married to or who gave her birth but by the person who lived inside. One of the things that I will continue to empower myself and others with is the power that God allowed me to see we have an inheritance that is based on Overcoming what we have been programmed to believe to being Elevated to His Purpose.

In my conclusion at this time, let me tell you that Overcoming to Elevate is a continuous process that we must continue to tackle. God allows that place of picking ourselves back up and dusting off the residue of uncertainty and even inadequacy. He allows us that place of safety in His arms that even when the walls comes shattering down and your glass house is in many pieces you can Overcome the pain to Elevate. The more we practice the steps the more we pray and seek His face the more we are becoming our true Unapologetic self to ourselves. Everyone else will figure it out but we have now stepped over to Overcoming to Elevate. I do not know about you my friend, but I smell our growth in this Elevation. Until we meet again my beloved.

Authentic Strategies Notes

Name

Date

_____

_____

_____

_____

_____

_____

_____

_____

_____

_____

_____

_____

_____

Authentic Strategies Notes

Name

Date

_____

_____

_____

_____

_____

_____

_____

_____

_____

_____

_____

_____

_____

_____

Authentic Strategies Notes

Name

Date

_____

_____

_____

_____

_____

_____

_____

_____

_____

_____

_____

_____

Chapter 5

SPIRITUAL SOUL WELLNESS COACHES

Shifting Gears With Grace

Kyonna F. Brown

The evening was made just for him and me. It was date night, and we were going to hit the pavement with one of his project cars. My husband has a knack for restoring older cars. Now, some of the vehicles I would not dare want to be caught dead in until he restores them. I like the finished polished look and he likes the broken-up piece of metal that he sees a vision for. Once he has them fixed, he likes to show me all the hard work he has completed. He also has a need for speed and honestly, it scares me sometimes, but I still ride. I just use my imaginary brakes on the passenger side floor board. This evening, we took out the 300zx. It was a nice summer evening. Just the right amount of heat mixed with a breeze. He removed the "T" shaped top off the car so we could ride topless. I had my shades on and he had his swag on. We were ready to enjoy the ride and one another. The car was a manual vehicle. This means that in order to go he had to shift from one gear to the next. As we hit the highway, he shifted from the lowest gear to the highest to gain speed and momentum. With each gear shift there was only a certain time limit to stay in that gear before he shifted again. He did it so gracefully, and with each shift, it was a smooth transition. I would not have noticed the gear change if I hadn't been watching him. As I sat back in thought to write this chapter that night came to mind. It reminded me of how I lost myself because of my need for speed. I did not shift gears gracefully. I went full throttle.

In 2017, I was introduced to the world of coaching, authorship, public speaking, network marketing, and various other ways to have multiple streams of income. At that time, I was already a business owner with a brick and mortar called Pooch Styles Pet Grooming. I had already had a taste of what entrepreneurship looked like. I already knew the freedom it posed, also the sleepless nights and long days that it came with as well. I saw the potential change in my life status as it referred to man and not God. Initially I prayed about joining a book collaboration. After that, I honestly assumed that God was in every decision after that, and he was not. My past was not all roses or a walk in a park. More like roses who were not tended to on the rough side of the mountain. I was incarcerated for 4 years due to a life of youthful brokenness, drug addiction, low self-esteem, and lack of forgiveness. In that season, I grew from broken to mended. After that time away from home, family, friends, and I vowed not to let myself go back down that road again. Hence my need for growth in every area of my life. That journey became the catalyst for who most people know me as today. "The Forgiveness Expert!" My mission is to share the massive message of forgiveness throughout the world. It was the start to my healing and gave me a new walk.

I was introduced to sharing my journey to help others. Immediately I met some of the world's top coaches. I was off to a great start. Being an entrepreneur, I was well aware that in order to grow I had to invest. Invest in yourself they'd say. Therefore, I did, and I did, and I did. One of my coaches called me an information junkie. Now, she said it out of love, but it still stung. She told me it was now time to start implementing what I have already learned. I can honestly say that I had great coaches, but there were some who were just out for a check. They all made it sound so simple. Here's the model of success. Do this and you will get there. Show up every time, network, and get the big-ticket item. Well, it became draining going to everything, networking, and trying to gain what success. You see, we often hold success to the level or standard of what someone else has achieved. Today I have to obtain what success looks like for me and not anyone else. But let me slow down…. I'm getting ahead of myself.

I soon realized that after all the rat race wheel activity that the reason I was not excelling was that I was not organically growing. I was being man made and not tapping into the source. I was no longer connected to the vine. I did not seek God for authorization. John 15:5 in the Bible states it well, "I am the vine, you are the branches. He who abides in Me, and I in him, bears much (E) fruit; for without Me you can do (F) nothing. Because I was not connected my fruit was not growing, meaning all the work I was doing really didn't go anywhere. In order for me to truly advance I needed to be connected to the true source. All things that grow have roots. When we detach ourselves, we are not able to grow organically. You might be asking yourself, about your roots. We grow or become stagnant because of the vines we are attached to. Family, friends, environments, and failure are some roots that help us propel or stand still. Who and what we choose to connect to can determine our outcome professionally, emotionally, and spiritually.

Although I prayed for answers and solutions in the journey, I did not wait for answers. I believed that I had to be attached to everything and everyone that would make my growth happen faster. After all, I had bills to pay and I needed more sustainability than my own business offered. As time went on, I spent time away from my family and I'd even spent lessor time with God. After all, working pretty much 7 days a week, having the day job with all my evening work, weekend conferences, and even traveling, who could really spend that much intimate time with God. That is what I told myself anyway. Besides, in my mind I believed He blessed me with all of those things anyway. I'd wish I could redeem the time. Wishing for more time but I was spending my time all on the wrong things. It's just like spending your money on junk food eating it and expecting healthy results. It's just not going to happen. I needed to change who I was connected to, and the need for speed. The scripture that changed my life is….

Galatians 6:8 | NIV - Whoever sows to please their flesh, from the flesh will reap destruction; whoever sows to please the Spirit, from the Spirit will reap eternal life.

In my need for speed, I became detached from sowing into the kingdom. Sowing my time in relationships with God to receive divine direction. Destruction was happening all around me. This was a result of believing in man and not the creator. I have learned that we all have gifts and talents. Most of us confuse the two as the same. I definitely did. A gift is something that you don't have to work towards, and your talent is something that you do. Being lost in that definition caused me to put in more effort for talent and not work in my God given gift. When we are working outside of our gifts, we sometimes put more strain on ourselves than needed. Let me ask you this question. Have you a need for speed? Have you been putting more into a talent than your gift? Have you been disconnected from the vine? Have you lost your intimacy with God? I want you to know that all pressures can end by simply asking for forgiveness. Forgiveness comes with admittance of your truth. The earnest desire to let go and the desire for total healing. You see, sometimes we have to be like my husband, see the brokenness before the beauty and take our time getting to greatness. Man-made success will only last a season, but God graced success will make your name great eternally. Let's look at faith and hope. Most of the time what I thought was faith was only hope. I hoped so much that I thought it was faith. Hebrews 11:1 - King James Version

11 Now faith is the substance of things hoped for, the evidence of things not seen. A lot of what I wanted I'd seen before. It was not until my very last coach wanted me to lie. Yes, I

lied. They wanted me to allude to the false truth of being totally healed. I know what connected me to others is pure authenticity. I was not willing to sell my soul for a dollar. By this time, I had invested $1000.00's of dollars into myself and I felt like I was not where this coaching company said I would be. I prayed about my dissatisfaction with this organization and I was moved to release all ties with the coach. I questioned God and it seemed as if it was an audible voice in my head saying very firmly "LEAVE IT ALONE." If you were near me, you might have thought I was crazy because I responded "okay". Honestly praying and being connected to the vine for divine instruction was the best choice I could have made. Following what I believe to be God's orders have changed my life dramatically. I actually even went back to God asking Him to provide me with at least two speaking engagements per month. Can I tell you; God has done it? I just had to reconnect to the vine. My need for speed has changed. I am now taking my time and letting only God advance me. No fuller throttle. I am doing this thing with grace. My faith is no longer a hope. God is doing things in my life that I have never imagined myself doing. My true faith came with operating attached to the kingdom. That took work. Believing not what the world says I should be but who God said I am. Scripture tells us "For as the body without the spirit is dead, so faith without works is also dead." James 2:26. I am no longer dead. I am alive. I am shifting gears with grace. A movie director, creator, and storyteller are who I am. I share inspirational films about forgiveness and healing. Where have you been speeding? If we slow down, we will be able to see more of the scenery that life has to offer. Remember you were graced for this.

"In You, O LORD, I put my trust; Let me never be put to shame. Deliver me in Your righteousness and cause me to escape; Incline your ear to me and save me. Be my strong refuge, to which I may resort continually; You have given the commandment to save me, For You are my rock and my fortress. Deliver me, O my God, out of the hand of the wicked, Out of the hand of the unrighteous and cruel man. For You are my hope, O Lord GOD; You are my trust from my youth. By You I have been upheld from birth; You are He who took me out of my mother's womb. My praise shall be continually of You. I have become as a wonder to many, But You are my strong refuge. Let my mouth be filled with Your praise And with Your glory all day. Do not cast me off in the time of old age; Do not forsake me when my strength fails. For my enemies speak against me; And those who lie in wait for my life take counsel together, Saying, "God has forsaken him; Pursue and take him, for there is none to deliver him." O God do not be far from me; O my God, make haste to help me! Let them be confounded and consumed Who are adversaries of my life; Let them be covered with reproach and dishonor Who seek my hurt. But I will hope continually and will praise You yet more and more. My mouth shall tell of Your righteousness And Your salvation all day, For I do not know their limits. I will go in the strength of the Lord GOD; I will make mention of Your righteousness, of Yours only. O God, you have taught me from my youth; And to this day I declare Your wondrous works. Now also when I am old and gray headed, O God, do not forsake me, Until I declare Your strength to this generation, your power to everyone who is to come. Also, your righteousness, O God, is very high, you who have done great things; O God, who is like You? You, who have shown me great and severe troubles, shall revive me again, and bring me up again from the depths of the earth. You shall increase my greatness, And comfort me on every side. Also, with the lute I will praise You— And Your faithfulness, O my God! To You I will sing with the harp, O Holy One of Israel. My lips shall greatly rejoice when I sing to You, and my soul, which You have redeemed. My tongue also shall talk of Your righteousness all day long; For they are confounded, for they are brought to shame Who seek my hurt."

Psalms 71:1-24 NKJV

God's Timing Is Always Perfect

Pastor Mike Kabia

Jesus said to him "IF YOU CAN BELIEVE. ALL THINGS ARE POSSIBLE TO HIM THAT BELIEVES (Mark 9:23). One of the hardest things I have found myself having to do as a Pastor is putting my Faith into action for a favorable outcome when life seems to show me everything but faith. The ability to stay in the realm of faith versus reason has caused many people to miss mighty moves of God. Jesus reminded us in Matthew 13:58 how he could not do many mighty works because of their unbelief. The ability to believe past what we see when we find ourselves in the midst of the fiery furnaces of life. Some of the time, it just does not make sense and can cause people to lean on their own understanding.

In this process, the enemy is relentlessly bombarding you with different scenarios about what could go wrong. Including the thought of what will not happen; putting your faith in action will have you at times looking crazy. This may be a scene replayed just like Noah. Noah was given the task of building an Ark to prepare for a flood that was going to come by rain. However, just imagine it had never rained before on Earth. I can only imagine the ridicule he faced from people every day because he chose to stand on the Word of God that he received firsthand notification from God Almighty. How are you standing? Noah decided not to allow the perceptions of others to stop him from putting his faith in action. Like so many of us do allow the perceptions of others stop us for putting our faith in action. To God be the glory Noah did not let that stop him. He had enough to believe God despite what logically didn't make sense. The bible is filled with numerous testimonies of what happened when people decided to put their faith in action and have "SIGHT" beyond what they see. Your back may be against the wall and you may not see your way out, but I challenge you to "PUT YOUR FAITH IN ACTION" no matter what. Continue to trust in the one who promises to deliver us from all of our fears, troubles, and afflictions. Let your faith cause mountains to move.

Some Principles Steps of Faith:

✓ Seek God's Counsel before other people's opinion
✓ Let the Holy Spirit lead the way
✓ Focus on what you will gain not lose

Authentic Strategies Notes

Name

Date

_____

_____

_____

_____

_____

_____

_____

_____

_____

_____

_____

_____

Authentic Strategies Notes

Name

Date

_____

_____

_____

_____

_____

_____

_____

_____

_____

_____

_____

_____

Authentic Strategies Notes

Name

Date

_____

_____

_____

_____

_____

_____

_____

_____

_____

_____

_____

_____

MEET THE AUTHORS

Michelle Boulden Hammond Visionary

Michelle Boulden Hammond is a multitalented woman who God has placed many gifts within her to inspire others. She handles her marriage, business and professional relationships with the power of integrity. Michelle also diligently works with her creativeness as an Author, Life Coach, Psalmist and Podcast host of Upfront Mind Body & Soul which can be heard weekly on Thursday evenings. As a leading lady of inspiration, she has traveled nationally and internationally doing women empowerment conferences called "Warm Your Heart; Warm Your Mind & Warm Your Soul." In this capacity, over 800 women have been served within the twelve years that this ministry has flourished. She is a small-town girl from Unionville on Maryland's Eastern Shore. A descendant of one of the Ex-18 Union Slaves who served in the Civil War. In 2016 she was the first African American woman in Talbot County, MD to open a wellness center that helped with the initiatives of health disparities for people of color. Michelle believes that purpose builds legacy and Legacy brings value to integrity. She resides in Caroline County, MD with her husband Elvis.

Website: www.upfrontmindbodysoul.com

Email: upfrontmbs@gmail.com

Tune in Every Thursday for Upfront Mind Body & Soul 6pm Weekly

Elite Conversations: https://bit.ly/UpfrontMindSoulPodcast

iHeart Radio: https://bit.ly/UpfrontMindSoulPodcast-iHeartRadio

Apple Podcast: https://bit.ly/UpfrontMindSoulPodcast-ApplePodcast

Bernadette Brawner

As Chief Executive Officer of BB Coaching and Consulting, Bernadette's personal and professional life has exemplified the powerful result of what happens when an individual perseveres, strives for more, and consistently moves forward despite their circumstances. Personally, her confidence and strength has grown and evolved to the point where she now empowers others through BB Coaching and Consulting and her nonprofit organization, Sisters Helping Empower Each Other (SHEE). As a single mother, despite the odds against her, she was able to raise a daughter who she has an unbelievable relationship with one of the victories she acknowledges as one of her greatest achievements.

As a Certified Life Coach, Bernadette also holds a Master of Business Administration (MBA) degree. She is Federal Triangle Club Immediate Past Toastmasters President, a facilitator, motivational speaker, and a community volunteer. Her published books, S.H.E.E. Prayer Devotional, provides women everywhere with the practical steps to experiencing God's best now! Her latest published book, Women Inspiring Nations WIN

II, Ms. Brawner is a co-author sharing her story of a single mother's triumph from struggle to success. Of all her many accomplishments, it is her faith in God's Word that is the driving force for success.

Dr. Jennifer Jones Bryant

Dr. Jennifer Jones Bryant is the Executive Founder of Reaching Within, An Empowerment Journey LLC, Best Selling Author, Award Winning Certified Life Coach, Career Strategist, Mentor, and International Speaker. She helps women accelerate to the next level in their career. She has over 25 years of demonstrated expertise helping individuals and teams in the federal government and corporate become high performers and more marketable through her leadership. Her educational background and personal experiences have given her a broad base from which to help clients find their inner strength to create and revise their personal and professional journey in life to achieve results. She influences others through her Empowerment Journey Podcast where others share their stories of overcoming personal and professional challenges to live their lives unashamed, unapologetically, and confidently. In addition to Dr. Jennifer appearing on TV, podcasts, and being featured in global magazines, she regularly receives speaking invitations from federal agencies, academia, and community organizations.

Joi Brown

Joi Brown is known as a Career Strategist, Life Coach, Fitness Instructor, Professor, Administrator, and Entrepreneur. Joi continues to fulfill her life's motto *"If I can help somebody along this journey called life with a word or song, then my living will not be in vain"* through her professional and community endeavors.

Joi is recognized as a human resource development and management expert possessing over twenty-one years in the Federal Government. She is the Chief Executive Officer of 3EEE Consulting, where she continues to help people strategize way to obtain a healthy, holistic, and purposeful life through customized services, conversations and dialogues, and workshops and presentations. Joi's impact and presence are felt by others through her coaching and mentorship in career and job coaching, goal setting and attainment, health, wellness and wellness, image branding, life skills, conflict to collaboration, and life transitions.

Joi is an advocate for spiritual and physical empowerment and personal development. As a Zumba and MixxedFit Instructor since 2012, she motivates and inspires others to be active and live their best life. Joi's classes are high energy with easy-to-follow choreographed steps and upbeat music that create a party atmosphere. Joi believes: "In every Small Step you take, you will see Big Results!"

Joi is a certified Treasury Executive Institute Coach and Integrative Wellness and Life Coach and continues to make an impact in the lives of future HR practitioners as an Adjunct Professor at her alma mater Bowie State University.

Deeply involved in public service and community organizations: Prince George's County Alumnae Chapter of Delta Sigma Theta Sorority, Community of Hope AME Church, and Toiletry in Company, Inc., Joi is the proud mother of Eagle Scout Javonte' P. Brown who recently graduated from Virginia State University, Class of 2020.

Foremost, Joi is walking in her purpose and using her God-given gifts and talents to help others live their best life.

Instagram: @3eeeconsulting or 3eeeconsulting@gmail.com

Kyonna F. Brown

Uplift Women Alliance's (UWA) founder and visionary, Kyonna F. Brown is the forgiveness expert and a God-graced woman with a story - one that runs layers deep, including a four-year sentence in a maximum-security prison; one that is loaded with revelation, triumph and nuggets of wisdom; one that is grounded in forgiveness and service. Kyonna utilizes her forgiveness strategies on multiple platforms. For UWA, she is poised to serve, support and equip women who are wearing layers of hurt, pain & unforgiveness - issues when left unaddressed builds up enough power to keep them stuck, functioning in dysfunction and bitter. Through UWA, she serves as lead navigator for those ready to walk the path to forgiveness, discover their purpose and establish authentic confidence so they can live as pure B.O.L.D.

Her vision for each member of UWA is a personalized navigation to their destiny through three steps: Get out their T.R.A.P (TOXIC mindset. REJECTION. Being AFRAID. In PAIN). Step in their P.O.D. (Point of Disruption designed for self-discovery and repossession of purpose). Live as pure B.O.L.D. (Believer. Overcomer. Leader. Destinygrabber). "When you are able to forgive, there is freedom & confidence that emerges which makes serving [voluntarily or with your business] seem effortless."

Kyonna is also a media guru, successful business owner and an established author. She wrote Blessed Hands: The Pathway to Forgiveness, and contributed to Breaking Free Forever, The Momentous Journey, and Break Through featuring Les Brown and other authors. She is a field correspondent for His Favor Magazine, which has showcased Tamala Mann and Joyce Myers; and is the former host of Urban Style Media's Forgiveness Friday, a weekly highly demanded evening show dedicated to commanding constant life issues with her forgiveness strategies. Determined to release women from all walks of life, Kyonna recently became a CMAT prison mentor. She also has stepped into the world of developing short films with Forgiveness Nation Media (UWA). Bringing the community together as actors and actresses to deliver the message of forgiveness with storytelling through film production. Pooch Styles, her trendy creative pet grooming & aesthetician business in the DMV, is where she and her staff offer FURgiveness to 4-legged members of various families. Based on her observing a community of pet owners ill equipped to properly recognize and respond to their pet grooming needs, she provides tips and tools via her book How to care for the pet I love.

Above all else, Kyonna enjoys serving her great husband Charles, nurturing and developing their son, Jeremiah and taking ultimate care of their three fur babies Kyndal, KoKo and Bella. Connect with her & follow her on Facebook and Instagram at theforgivenessexpert.

Shawna Halley

To Restore the Goddess Identity Within; is to Value your Vision.

As a Certified Life & Business Evolution Strategist, National Transformational Success Speaker, Chief Confidence Builder, Author-Poet, Shawna has strategically coached over 150 individuals since 2018 by way of group and individual sessions. *She is passionate about showing women how to RISE...to enter into a passionate love affair with themselves & prosperous living daily...they RISE out of shame, blame, guilt, scarcity; and prepare their minds to tune into the hearts' desires.*

She promotes conscious collaboration and connection to creatively…

"Make our presence

and our contribution

a generational GIFT to Nations"

Shawn's journey from disillusion to positive envisioning, makes her the ideal Transformative Life & Business Evolution Strategist to assist you in valuing your vision to build your dreams; thereby, transforming your life, **ALL** on your terms.

'Your' TRUTH! Your time matters let us not delay, nor waste it-invest it instead.

What I love about our journey together is we going to have lots of fun. Allowing yourself to feel love's presence is your ultimate soul connection. This embodiment will release and increase rapid awakening, restoration and ascension to your inner love, light, beauty and truth…. Are you ready Divine Goddess…Let's Go!!!

Victoria Holland

Evangelist Victoria Holland is a native of Martinsville, VA and currently resides in Greensboro, NC. She is the youngest daughter of Elder Edward Holland and the late First Lady Nannie Holland. Evangelist Holland is the proud parent of three beautiful daughters: Kristy, Katina, and Tamika Redd all of Greensboro, NC and three grandsons, Trenton, Jesiah and Julian. She has three beautiful godchildren.

She is the Founder and Facilitator of Victoria Elevates LLC which is the Umbrella that covers Elevated Not Tolerated Coaching & Motivational Services, Elegant Elevations Floral Designs, Anointed New Dreams (AND) and a host of other arising businesses. Victoria is a Certified Master Life Coach with numerous ranges of specific expertise, and her favorite is ELEVATION AND MOTIVATION.

In 2019, Victoria created and taught her phenomenal course. "The Positive Self Building Course" which empowers individuals to build the real person on the inside and to flourish on the outside through basic skill and mindset techniques. She created the name "The Elevated Not Tolerated Academy" for the students to have their very own "school" of learning. In July 2020 in the middle of the Pandemic, the 1st graduating class walked across the virtual stage.

Evangelist Holland, a powerful and anointed woman of God was given the vision for the ministry in February 2005. She preached her initial sermon in March 2005 & the ministry has been formed & in consistent construction since the vision was given with her style and personality, Evangelist Holland has a unique and amazing way of reaching her audience and relaying the word of God. She believes in equipping the saints and evangelizing the sinner whenever the opportunity is presented itself.

She is a family-oriented and a positive individual who just simply loves God with everything she has. She is a true leader, motivator, conqueror, and teacher. Her praise is out of this world and her worship is for real.

Dr. Mary J. Huntley

I am the Chief Executive Officer of an exclusive consulting organization. Motivation, integrity and professionalism are a few of my company values. I have been married for 46 years and I am honored to serve as Executive Director of an NCCA Certified Academic Institute. I am a 2019 Indy Author Legacy Award Winner, 3X International and 8X Bestselling Author, Board Certified Master Motivational Mindset Coach and a Domestic Violence Advocate. I am also a Licensed Professional Counselor with Advanced Certifications in Death and Grief Therapy, Group Therapy, Integrated Marriage and Family Therapy, Cognitive Therapy, and Crisis and Abuse Therapy. I am a Clinical Supervisor, and a Professional Clinical member with the National Christian Counselors, and a Certified Temperament Coach with the Sarasota Academy of Christian Counselors. I am a Platinum Member of Vocalizers Women Speakers Academy Certified Training Program under the auspices of international motivational speaker Dr. Cheryl Wood.

I am a modern-day Harriet Tubman "called" to serve the hurting, rejected and unnoticed. I am on assignment to free individuals from the chains that enslave their minds, as I empower them by raising low self-esteem. I teach them that you can live amid poverty and possess a rich mentality that provides an escape route. I also serve as an advocate for those who find themselves in a holding pattern while awaiting their next move toward destiny. In essence, my assignment is to use my life experiences to walk you through the maze of life with the blessed assurance that you will reach your destiny.

Contact Information: drmaryjhuntley.com

Sheila Gibson

Sheila Gibson-Cornett served in the Federal Government for over 33 years. She has a degree in Paralegal Studies and a master's degree in business administration. She has experience in consulting with the Non-Profit industry. She also is a business owner of SAM Consulting advising and sharing information on Estate Planning and Notary Public. She specializes in advising how to write a Last Will and Testament and Power of Attorney. She has been an awesome blessing to the body of Christ. In her servitude in ministry, she has provided the services as Administrator, Advisor, Trustee Board Representative, and Church Secretary. All things have been done in excellence for the Lord. In her spare time, she likes to partake in graphic design as a hobby.

Ms. Gibson-Cornett has a reputation for stellar performances, organizational skills and attention to details along with self-motivation. She is a mother of three daughters and one granddaughter. Her words of encouragement to individuals are: "never take our freedom for granted." She has earned the love and respect from all that she has helped. She wants health, happiness, and prosperity to everyone she meets. Her favorite scripture is Psalm 23.

Contact Information

samconsultingrequest@gmail.com

Linkedin.com/in/Sheila-gibson-08793a77

Pastor Mike Kabia

Pastor Mike Kabia, is an anointed powerful man who is on a mission of servitude for the Lord. Pastor Mike is the Senior Pastor of It's My Time Ministries located in Washington, DC. Pastor Mike is a faithful servant who diligently serves those who are less fortunate in the streets. He has hosted numerous homeless outreaches in the heart of District of Columbia 425 2nd Street NW. Pastor Mike holds weekly and daily morning spiritual vitamins for the soul on Facebook Live. He quotes "God's Timing Is Always Perfect."

Contact Info: blkmike2k2@yahoo.com

Lynda D. Mallory

Lynda D. Mallory is from Beltsville, Maryland and she is a writer, blogger, and a published author at A Life with A View. She inspires people to write creatively and with purpose. Lynda is inspired by stories of faith, love, and happiness and by people who embrace their journey with the courage and the passion to be successful in life. She has two wonderful children, Miles and Madison, and she adores their creative spirits. You can find Lynda at A Life With A View everywhere and on her website is: www.lyndadmallory.com

Charlene Harrod-Owuamana

Charlene Harrod-Owuamana is a Best-selling Author, Professional Speaker and Educator to youth, in Baltimore City. She started her business as a "Kid's Coach" for her personal Brand "Nursz's HIVE & CEO/Founder of Owuamana Enterprise, LLC.

Nursz's HIVE, inspires youth from ages 8 to 24 years old - to focus on a Career in Healthcare. There are many occupations and career choices in healthcare. She teaches and educates the youth to prepare them for their future. She has been in the Healthcare System for over 36+ years. With 20+ years as a Licensed Practical Nurse (LPN), she graduated from Baltimore County Community Colleges (Essex Campus) with an Associate of Science Degree.

She serves on several boards in her city such as: Black Girls Vote (BGV) and Maryland Board of Nursing (CNA Advisory Committee), where she holds several board seats. She is a Delegate for the 2020 Ms. Exquisite Full-Figured DMV Pageant. She is published in several magazines, such as Entrepreneur 2018 Washington D.C. Edition by Trends and Empowering. Some of her accomplishments include: speaking at "Baltimore in Conversation" on Trust VS Mistrust in Healthcare with LGBTQ community, two-time

Speaker at "NursesTakeDC"; Former/Founder of Black Nurses Rock – Baltimore Maryland Chapter, where she changed lives by educating the communities in which she served. An author and co-author of several non-fiction and Christian books.

Despite all the challenges that her city has been faced with over the years. She returned to the neighborhood where she was raised after 40 years. To strengthen the Healthcare System and show the community her commitment and dedication. She managed to collaborate with top city leaders and educators, such as, Baltimore City Mayors Office, Baltimore City Fire Department and others. Remaining busy in vulnerable communities doing what God intended her to be nurturing, caring and inspiring Nurse.

I AM A NURSE!

One of the lessons that I grew up with was to always stay true to yourself and never let what somebody else says distract you from your goals. Therefore, when I hear about negative and false attacks, I do not invest any energy in them. Because I know who I am.

Milagros Richards

Milagros Mercedes Richards, known as Millie Richards in the entertainment, Health and Fitness World, Milagros De Las Mercedes Sanchez Paga, later Milagros Mercedes Santiago Pagan, Born on January 4th, 1971 in Manhattan, New York. She is the artistic child of Mercedes Pagan Sellas and raised by Angel Luis Santiago Agricourt. Eight years after my birth, we moved to my parent's birth land Puerto Rico where I lived until the age of 21. During those years, I participated in school plays, took Modeling and etiquette training, went to the school of performing arts where I learned to play the flute, the clarinet, and learned some singing. Went to elementary Schools, Middle Schools, and High Schools, and almost two years of College in Puerto Rico.

Life Coach, Model, MC, Public Speaker, Jewelry designer, Acting Talent on the "RISE TO FAME", "DRAGON SQUAD" Mini-series. I am of Puerto Rican descent and loves life. Fully trained in CPR, FIRST Aid AED, Lifeguard, water fitness, Voice over, Human

Relation skills, Kung Fu, Action Film, I love the RUNWAY MODELING and love, fashion with a cause.

Work/Awards: Urban Action showcases, New York City 2019, and 2020. Published by AMAZING magazine Dec. 2019, January 2020, MC at CMG New York Fashion Week 2019, Editorial Model for the worldwide AMAZING magazine 2019 and 2020. Won first place at Discover Me Showcase USA Trendsetter 1st Place Runway, TV, Commercial, and Photography (trendsetter) 1st Place group runway competition, 2nd Runner up legs competition, 3rd runner up Soap star acting at MAAI Miami, FL in June 2018.

You can follow me on social media at:

- https://www.facebook.com/pg/MilagrosRichardsfanpage/photos/?tab=albums&ref=page_internal
- https://www.instagram.com/richardsmilagros
- https://www.youtube.com/channel/UC0Iuj24txi26WEOkFVsSi7w Milagros Richards Step into Change

Team of Authentic Coaches

FOREWORD BY DR. MARY J. HUNTLEY

SILHOUETTES OF STRATEGIES FROM AUTHENTIC COACHES FOR MIND, BODY & SOUL

VISIONARY MICHELLE BOULDEN-HAMMOND

Visionary
MICHELLE BOULDEN-HAMMOND

Foreword Author
DR. MARY J. HUNTLEY

BERNADETTE BRAWNER

JOI BROWN

KYONNA T. BROWN

DR. JENNIFER BRYANT

SHEILA GIBSON

SHAWNA HALLEY

CHARLENE HARROD-OWUAMANA

VICTORIA HOLLAND

PASTOR MIKE KABIA

LYNDA D. MALLORY

MILAGROS M. RICHARDS

SILHOUETTES OF STRATEGIES FROM AUTHENTIC COACHES FOR MIND, BODY & SOUL

Special Thanks

I want to first thank God again for placing his gift of creativeness within me. I want to take time to acknowledge and thank all the contributors to this special project called "Silhouettes of Strategies From Authentic Coaches For Mind, Body & Soul". It is awesome when authentic individuals come together to share their expertise for the community. This is a general enterprise of wealth coming from some amazing, phenomenal Certified Coaches that not only execute strategies but love helping others move into their full potential.

I want to express my true measure of gratitude for all that answered call. Dr. Mary J. Huntley for enlightening my fire in the beginning stages. My Co-Authors Bernadette Brawner, Joi Brown, Kyonna F. Brown, Dr. Jennifer Jones Bryant, Sheila Gibson, Shawna Halley, Victoria Holland, Pastor Mike Kabia, Lynda D. Mallory, Charlene Harrod-Owuamana, Milagros Richards. Thank you, and my prayers that God continues to bless each of you in your continual prosperous journeys of life.

www.ingramcontent.com/pod-product-compliance
Lightning Source LLC
Chambersburg PA
CBHW081158270326
41930CB00014B/3208